Mother,
   Here's something
to help us prepare
our hearts for the
miracle of Christmas.

♥ Julie

2003

Watch for the Light

Watch for the Light

Readings for Advent and Christmas

PLOUGH PUBLISHING HOUSE

Published by The Plough Publishing House
of The Bruderhof Foundation, Inc., Farmington PA 15437 USA
and by Bruderhof Communities in the UK,
Robertsbridge, East Sussex TN32 5DR UK

06 05 04 03 02   10 9 8

A catalog record for this book is available from the British Library.

Library of Congress Cataloging-in-Publication Data

Watch for the light : readings for Advent and Christmas.
    p. cm.
  Includes bibliographical references and index.
  ISBN 0-87486-917-X (alk. paper)
  1. Advent--Meditations. 2. Christmas--Meditations.   I. Plough Publishing
House.
  BV40 .W295 2001
  242'.33--dc21

                    2001004753

Printed in the USA

Lo, in the silent night
A child to God is born
And all is brought again
That ere was lost or lorn.

Could but thy soul, O man,
Become a silent night!
God would be born in thee
And set all things aright.

15TH CENTURY

Each selection in this book stands on its own. Dates in the upper margin have been provided for those who wish to follow the readings sequentially, on a daily basis.

Advent begins on a different date each year, but this book begins early enough (November 24) to be used regardless of the liturgical calendar. It ends with a reading for the day after Epiphany (January 6), which is the traditional close of the holidays.

Contents

CONTENTS

CONTENTS

ix

CONTENTS

x

CONTENTS

Introduction

Light your candles quietly, such candles as you possess, wher-
ever you are.

ALFRED DELP

THOUGH ADVENT (literally "arrival") has been observed for centuries as a time to contemplate Christ's
birth, most people today acknowledge it only with a
blank look. For the vast majority of us, December
flies by in a flurry of activities, and what is called
"the holiday season" turns out to be the most stress-
ful time of the year.

It is also a time of contrasting emotions. We are
eager, yet frazzled; sentimental, yet indifferent. One
minute we glow at the thought of getting together
with our family and friends; the next we feel utterly
lonely. Our hope is mingled with dread, our antici-

pation with despair. We sense the deeper meanings of the season but grasp at them in vain; and in the end, all the bustle leaves us frustrated and drained.

Even we who do not experience such tensions – who genuinely love Christmas – often miss its point. Content with candles and carols and good food, we bask in the warmth of familiar traditions, in reciprocated acts of kindness, and in feelings of general goodwill. How many of us remember the harsh realities of Christ's first coming: the dank stable, the cold night, the closed door of the inn? How many of us share the longing of the ancient prophets, who awaited the Messiah with such aching intensity that they foresaw his arrival thousands of years before he was born?

Mother Teresa once noted that the first person to welcome Christ was John the Baptist, who leaped for joy on recognizing him, though both of them were still within their mothers' wombs. We, in stark contrast, are often so dulled by superficial distractions that we are incapable of hearing any voice within, let alone listening to it. Consequently, the feeling we know as Christmas cheer lacks any real connection to the vital spirit that radiated from the manger.

That is the main purpose of this collection: to re-forge that link, and to encourage the rediscovery of Advent as a season of inward preparation.

We miss the essence of Christmas unless we become, in the words of Eberhard Arnold, "mindful of how Christ's birth took place." Once we do, we will sense immediately that Advent marks something momentous: God's coming into our midst. That coming is not just something that happened in the past. It is a recurring possibility here and now. And thus Advent is not merely a commemorative event or an anniversary, but a yearly opportunity for us to consider the future, second Advent – the promised coming of God's kingdom on earth.

Such an understanding of Christmas is possible only insofar as we let go of the false props of convention and seek to unlock its central paradox. That paradox, to paraphrase the modern martyr Dietrich Bonhoeffer, is the fact that God's coming is not only a matter of glad tidings but, first of all, "frightening news for everyone who has a conscience."

The love that descended to Bethlehem is not the easy sympathy of an avuncular God, but a burning fire whose light chases away every shadow, floods every corner, and turns midnight into noon. This love reveals sin and overcomes it. It conquers darkness with such forcefulness and intensity that it scatters the proud, humbles the mighty, feeds the hungry, and sends the rich away empty-handed (Luke 1:51–53).

Because a transformation of this scale can never be achieved by human means, but only by divine intervention, Advent (to quote Bonhoeffer again) might be compared to a prison cell "in which one waits and hopes and does various unessential things… but is completely dependent on the fact that the door of freedom has to be opened from the outside." It is a fitting metaphor. But dependency does not release us from responsibility. If the essence of Advent is expectancy, it is also readiness for action: watchfulness for every opening, and willingness to risk everything for freedom and a new beginning.

That is why the imagery of nativity scenes is not sufficient to explain the Christmas message. Yes, God came into the feeding trough of an animal. But it was not only as a baby that he lay there. This child was the same man who was crucified on Golgotha, and who rose again. Within the manger lies the cross – and the hope of redemption and resurrection.

To recognize this requires reverence and humility. It requires faith. We might ask, "What grounds are there for such hope?" Or we might seek to become like children, and believe. Mary did. So did the shepherds and the wise men of the East. So did the men and women whose writings are gathered in this book. So can each of us, wherever we are.

THE EDITORS, ADVENT 2001

Action in Waiting

Christoph Friedrich Blumhardt

IT IS ADVENT AGAIN. We call this time Advent because it reminds us of what comes from God for the creation of his kingdom on earth. We who are here have been led in a special way to keep what is coming on our hearts and to shape ourselves according to it. That which comes from God – that is what moves our hearts, not only in these days but at all times. That which is to come from God is the most important thing we have, in the past and in the present as well as in the future. It is only in God's coming that even the Bible itself has value to us, let alone all the other things we call "means of grace." Unless what comes from God is a part of it, it remains like a dead seed and does not achieve what must be achieved if God's kingdom is to be.

There are many today who sigh to heaven, "Savior, come now!" But they are not sighing for the sake of God's kingdom. They cry out like this only when they are in trouble and want God to help them. And they don't know of any help that is more effective than to have a Savior come and put a quick end to their troubles.

When it comes to the things of God, however, we must not be concerned for what is ours, but only for what belongs to Christ. We should do this not merely for our own edification; we must become workers for God. This leads us to God's vineyard, a place where there is not a great deal of talk, but where everyone is intent on deeds.

This is what it means to prepare for Advent. Jesus says, "Be ready for action, and have your lamps lit; be like those who are waiting for their master to return from the wedding banquet…blessed is the slave whom his master will find at work when he arrives" (Luke 12:35–48). Here Jesus is speaking of his disciples and their preparation for his coming. Take note that God's kingdom is not formed by any human discovery or intention, however daring and noble, but by the coming of Christ. Our faith, our ardor, must be for this coming. Otherwise it would be better to put aside our meditations on Advent. The reign of God is a marvelous thing. To worldly wisdom God's kingdom seems like foolishness, and yet it gives shape to the whole world, the whole creation, making it God's eternal coming.

It is remarkable that not only God, creator of heaven and earth, but also God's people must be a part of this plan. There need to be men and women who give themselves up for God's kingdom and its justice. Otherwise Jesus would not have said, "Blessed are those servants whom the master finds awake when he comes." It is obvious that much depends on our activity. We can even read between the lines that if there is no one to watch out, God's coming will be delayed. Speaking in terms of the parable, if the doorkeeper does not open the door, it is possible that even the master himself, who has given him the key, cannot get in unless he forces his way.

There have to be people who, first of all, have dressed themselves for action and have lit their lamps. In other words, while their master is absent they are busy preparing everything in the house for his arrival and keeping everyone in the house aware that the state they are living in is only temporary.

Secondly, there must be people who stand by the door and listen for him and who open it quickly when he knocks. Workers, not slackers, are dressed for service. Slackers wear their Sunday best. A person who is getting ready to work with his hands takes his coat off and rolls up his sleeves so that he can get at the matter without further ado. God has work that has to be done in work clothes, not in one's Sunday best. As long as God's kingdom has to be fought for, it is more important to be dressed for work – ready for action – to make an effort to do something in keeping with God's plan, often against the whole weight of the world. A practical way exists and we must be ready for this with our whole being.

"But," someone may ask, "what sort of thing, exactly, are we to do? What will truly serve God and his coming reign?" That is a serious question; no human being can answer it. We have to learn to live in what is coming from God every day and to carry a light from this awareness into the darkness. For the essence of God's everlasting order has been darkened by the principalities and powers of this world. Throughout practically every realm of life there is an enslaving force. It is characteristic of everything, even the highest human undertakings of nations or of individuals; it is egoism. What can we get out of this or that? What will meet our momentary interest? We are only concerned with our immediate interest, and call this good and true. In this way the darkness comes.

We find it so difficult to put God's service into our daily life, but this is because we weak human beings don't really want to know what is true. We live in a mass of wrongs and untruths, and they surround us as a dark, dark night. Not even in the most flagrant things do we manage to break through. We are hardly repelled anymore by murder, adultery, or theft. We now have customs and laws under whose protection one person can kill another. We have lifestyles of pleasure that poison everything way beyond human help. We have customs of acquisitiveness by which some people live at the expense of others. What can be done to help?

Anyone whose attention is fixed on the coming reign of God and who wants to see a change brought about in God's house will become more and more aware that there exists a universal wrongness that is pulled over us like a choking, suffocating blanket. He will know that the thing to do is to take hold of God's hand so that there is some effect on this night, so that at least a few areas are made receptive to God's truth and justice and are made ready to receive God himself. But to do this work we have to have a light. With this light we can then illuminate every corner where we have some work to do. Then we will see where the garbage is, where there is work to be done.

This is really very hard work, but this is what preparing for Advent means. But look out! When someone holds a light in his hand and shines it here and there, he is immediately asked, "What business have you here?" Thus so many people let their light go out again. It is too awkward, too inconvenient to keep holding up a light and showing people the dirt and saying, "There, clean that up; the way you are doing things now isn't right in God's eyes. Cut off your hand! Tear out your eye! Cut off your foot!" – as Jesus says, figuratively, when there is something about the hand or eye or foot that stands in God's way.

"The light shines in darkness, and the darkness cannot overcome it." A light has a purpose; a light ought to shine into our lives so that we can see what needs to be done and set our hand to it and clean it up. Jesus, with this light, was not well received, and neither were his apostles. "If only that light weren't there," people said. In the times of the early church, the Christians were accused of causing confusion in the world, of undermining law and religion, and they were bitterly persecuted for this. The truth – the fact that people's lives are not right – is too much for most people to grasp. It seems like a crime to them to think that things they consider quite all right ought to be changed. The sacrifice of Christ, which makes it possible for a new humanity to arise in the resurrection – this sacrifice appears as foolishness.

So people turn finally to this Sunday religion and holiday worship. Going to worship is supposed to be enough. God is supposed to be satisfied with it and do without the weekday work. But let us not give the name of worship, or service to God, only to things that benefit us, only to things that soothe our own souls.

Fortunately, many people no longer feel that Sunday religion is enough. No matter how people talk, work clothes must come back. A new spirit is awakening, and there are many who seek for God's advantage, even though they may not know how to go about it. Others may polish themselves up spiritually to get their little souls in order for God. They can do this, but it is not enough. Anyone who has eyes will see this and consider how he can forget himself in devotion to God's kingdom and become ardent for the reign to come – to this he is called.

Closely connected with this first work is that of standing at the door and opening it. In regard to this work one often speaks of the first, second, or third watch; and, I would like to add, the fourth, the fifth, and the sixth. We must stand by the door constantly, ready to open it, even though there may be no knock for a long time. We must be prepared for the first, second, or third watch; even if it includes the fourth, the fifth, and the sixth watch.

Jesus came and departed. But his resurrection means that everything in God's kingdom is alive; in every moment there is something happening. He himself may yet come again; he may soon send a messenger to knock. When the door is opened he will say, "Listen, do this and that; tell the people in the house to watch out for this or that." Another time there is another knock, and the door is opened. This time perhaps the word is, "What is the foolishness you're doing in this house? You act as if things were going to always stay the same. Don't settle down as if you were the masters!" And this goes like the breath of God's wrath through the whole house, by way of the doorkeeper. Another time there is a knock, the doorkeeper opens, and the warning is heard, "Watch out for idolatry! Do you want to serve both God and mammon? Do you want to sit at both God's table and the demons' table? Who is your master? Do you want to work with the methods of this world or by the spirit of God? Truly, my house is not a house of human wisdom, but of God's."

For those who listen for Christ's coming, a knock sounds over and over again. The things that come forth are not necessarily highly spiritual. Sometimes they are very simple things. For instance, we may be told, "Don't neglect your bodies. Don't you know that your body is a temple of the Holy Spirit? (1 Cor. 3:16) Why do you drink so much wine? Why do you eat so much food?" This seems contemptibly small. Doesn't Paul say, "The kingdom of God does not consist in eating and drinking?" That is true. Yet for those who want to hear, there is a knock on the door for the coming future of Jesus Christ telling us to live for God in everything (1 Cor. 10:31). It is not only your souls that matter, but your bodies too. Whoever is wise will open the door when God's messengers speak about this. Whoever is wise will go at it joyfully and confidently.

We must speak in practical terms. Either Christ's coming has meaning for us now, or else it means nothing at all. Sometimes the knock has to do with our life together, or with the arrangements of our life in relationship to the world. For example, on a large estate there are managers, farmers, gardeners, cooks, and so on. The cook has learned cooking, the farmer farming, the gardener gardening, all according to the customary methods. They have learned their trades well and are able to carry them on, even to excel in them. But suppose there is a knock, the door is opened and they are told, "Listen now, don't simply keep house as the world does; stop and think how to do things so as to please me!" Maybe you will answer, "What do you mean? That's the way I learned it and that's how everybody else does it." True, everybody

does it that way; but you do not need to. Those intent on Christ's coming have to bring a different way
into their situations. Must things always be done in
the style of the world? (2 Cor. 10:3–4) According to
human wisdom? Should the kingdom of God run according to what most of us are used to?

A person who keeps watch for God, who lives for
his coming, will be glad to hear even about little
things like this, even if he is told, "Do everything
differently from the way you have been doing it till
now." When such a person hears the hint to do it
differently, he will stop and listen. He will ask, "Differently? How shall I do it differently?" First you will
have to become poor, and see where you have acted
foolishly, like someone who has no light. Then you
must grieve that you are not any cleverer than anyone else when it comes to opening the door to the
Master.

This is what it means to watch. We have to begin
with what we can see. Then there will come times
when we are allowed to watch in higher things. If
you look for the truth in small matters you will not
go astray in big ones. You will be able to recognize
truth there and carry out the command that comes.

Let us keep staunch in our eagerness to do whatever comes to us of the truth. Then there will be knocks on our door, over and over, and God's coming will not be hidden. For devoted hearts the light will keep dawning from him who is merciful and compassionate.

The work for God goes on quite simply in this way; one does not always have to wait for something out of the ordinary. The all-important thing is to keep your eyes on what comes from God and to make way for it to come into being here on the earth. If you always try to be heavenly and spiritually minded, you won't understand the everyday work God has for you to do. But if you embrace what is to come from God, if you live for Christ's coming in practical life, you will learn that divine things can be experienced here and now, things quite different from what our human brains can ever imagine.

Black Rook
in Rainy Weather

On the stiff twig up there
Hunches a wet black rook
Arranging and rearranging its feathers
    in the rain.
I do not expect a miracle
Or an accident

To set the sight on fire
In my eye, nor seek
Any more in the desultory weather
    some design,
But let spotted leaves fall as they fall,
Without ceremony, or portent.

Although, I admit, I desire,
Occasionally, some backtalk
From the mute sky, I can't honestly
    complain:
A certain minor light may still
Lean incandescent

Out of kitchen table or chair
As if a celestial burning took
Possession of the most obtuse objects
    now and then –
Thus hallowing an interval
Otherwise inconsequent

By bestowing largesse, honor,
One might say love. At any rate,
    I now walk
Wary (for it could happen
Even in this dull, ruinous landscape);
    skeptical,
Yet politic; ignorant

Of whatever angel may choose to flare
Suddenly at my elbow. I only know
   that a rook
Ordering its black feathers can so shine
As to seize my senses, haul
My eyelids up, and grant

A brief respite from fear
Of total neutrality. With luck,
Trekking stubborn through this season
Of fatigue, I shall
Patch together a content

Of sorts. Miracles occur,
If you dare to call those spasmodic
Tricks of radiance miracles. The wait's
   begun again,
The long wait for the angel,
For that rare, random descent.

SYLVIA PLATH

The Dangers of Advent

J. B. Phillips

BY FAR THE MOST IMPORTANT and significant event in the whole course of human history will be celebrated, with or without understanding, at the end of this season, Advent. The towering miracle of God's visit to this planet on which we live will be glossed over, brushed aside or rendered impotent by over-familiarity. Even by the believer the full weight of the event is not always appreciated. His faith is in Jesus Christ – he believes with all his heart that this man, who lived and died and rose again in Palestine, was truly the Son of God. He may have, in addition, some working experience that the man Jesus is still alive, and yet be largely unaware of the intense meaning of what he believes.

Does he, for instance, as he daily treads the surface of this planet, reflect with confidence that "my God has been here, here on this earth"? Does he keep his faith wrapped in a napkin as a precious thing and apart; or does he allow every discovery of the truth to enlarge his conception of the God behind this immensely complex universe? And does he then marvel and adore the infinite wisdom and power, which so humbly descends to human stature? We rejoice in the fact that God has actually been here – and that is one half of the meaning of Advent.

But there is another half. The eleven, who had had six weeks' experience of the risen Christ, were told after he had finally left their sight, that "this same Jesus shall so come in like manner as ye have seen him go."

As a translator of the New Testament I find in it no support whatever for the belief that one day all evil will be eradicated from the earth, all problems solved, and health and wealth be every man's portion! Even among some Christians such a belief is quite commonly held, so that the "second advent" of Christ is no more and no less than the infinite number of "comings" of Christ into men's minds. Of course, no one would deny that there are millions of such "comings" every year – but that is not what the Christian Church believes by the second advent of Christ; and it is most emphatically not what any writer of the New Testament ever meant in foretelling his second coming.

The New Testament is indeed a book full of hope, but we may search it in vain for any vague humanist optimism. The second coming of Christ, the second irruption of eternity into time, will be immediate, violent and conclusive. The human experiment is to end, illusion will give way to reality, the temporary will disappear before the permanent, and the king will be seen for who he is. The thief in the night, the lightning flash, the sound of the last trumpet, the voice of God's archangel – these may all be picture-language, but they are pictures of something sudden, catastrophic, and decisive. By no stretch of the imagination do they describe a gradual process.

I believe that the atheistic-scientific-humanist point of view is, despite its apparent humanitarianism, both misleading and cruel. In appearance it may resemble Christianity in that it would encourage tolerance, love, understanding, and the amelioration of human conditions. But at heart it is cruel, because it teaches that this life is the only life, that we have no place prepared for us in eternity, and that the only realities are those that we can appreciate in our present temporary habitation. Hence the current hysterical preoccupation with physical security, particularly in relation to the hydrogen bomb, which infects the lives of many professing Christians. When, we may well ask, have Christians been promised physical security? In the early Church it is evident that they did not even expect it! Their security, their true life, was rooted in God; and neither the daily insecurities of the decaying Roman Empire, nor the organized persecution which followed later, could affect their basic confidence.

In my judgement, the description which Christ gave of the days that were to come before his return is more accurately reproduced in this fear-ridden age than ever before in human history. Of course we do not know the times and the seasons, but at least we can refuse to be deceived by the current obsession for physical security in the here-and-now. While we continue to pray and work for the spread of the kingdom in this transitory world, we know that its center of gravity is not here at all. When God decides that the human experiment has gone on long enough, yes, even in the midst of what appears to us confusion and incompleteness, Christ will come again.

This is what the New Testament teaches. This is the message of Advent. It is for us to be alert, vigilant and industrious, so that his coming will not be a terror but an overwhelming joy.

According to an old saying, familiarity breeds contempt. Of course this is not always true! In particular, it is often not true of people with whom we are familiar. Indeed, with the best kind of friends, the more we know them, the more we grow to love and respect them. It is only the people who are superficial and at heart unreal who let us down when we grow familiar with them. It is then that our previous admiration can turn to contempt.

But the old saying was not intended to apply only to human relationships. There are situations where human beings are at first filled with awe, and then as they grow more and more familiar with them they experience first indifference, and then contempt. The "spiderman" who works on scaffolding hundreds of feet above the ground, has to be on his guard against this over-familiarity. The man who works with high-voltage electricity must also beware of becoming contemptuous of his danger. And anyone who knows the sea will say to you in effect, "By all means love the sea, but never lose your respect for it." Whenever familiarity breeds contempt there is potential danger.

The particular danger which faces us as Christmas approaches is unlikely to be contempt for the sacred season, but nevertheless our familiarity with it may easily produce in us a kind of indifference. The true wonder and mystery may leave us unmoved; familiarity may easily blind us to the shining fact that lies at the heart of Christmastide. We are all aware of the commercialization of Christmas; we can hardly help being involved in the frantic business of buying and sending gifts and cards. We shall without doubt enjoy the carols, the decorations, the feasting and jollification, the presents, the parties, the dancing and the general atmosphere of goodwill that almost magically permeates the days of Christmas. But we may not always see clearly that so much decoration and celebration has been heaped upon the festival that the historic fact upon which all the rejoicing is founded has been almost smothered out of existence.

What we are in fact celebrating is the awe-inspiring humility of God, and no amount of familiarity with the trappings of Christmas should ever blind us to its quiet but explosive significance. For Christians believe that so great is God's love and concern for humanity that he himself became a man. Amid the sparkle and the color and music of the day's celebration we do well to remember that God's insertion of himself into human history was achieved with an almost frightening quietness and humility. There was no advertisement, no publicity, no special privilege; in fact the entry of God into his own world was almost heartbreakingly humble. In sober fact there is little romance or beauty in the thought of a young woman looking desperately for a place where she could give birth to her first baby. I do not think for a moment that Mary complained, but it is a bitter commentary upon the world that no one would give up a bed for the pregnant woman – and that the Son of God must be born in a stable.

This almost beggarly beginning has been roman-ticized by artists and poets throughout the centuries. Yet I believe that at least once a year we should look steadily at the historic fact, and not at any pretty picture. At the time of this astonishing event only a handful of people knew what had happened. And as far as we know, no one spoke openly about it for thirty years. Even when the baby was grown to be a man, only a few recognized him for who he really was. Two or three years of teaching and preaching and healing people, and his work was finished. He was betrayed and judicially murdered, deserted at the end by all his friends. By normal human stan-dards this is a tragic little tale of failure, the rather squalid story of a promising young man from a humble home, put to death by the envy and malice of the professional men of religion. All this hap-pened in an obscure, occupied province of the vast Roman Empire.

It is fifteen hundred years ago that this apparently invincible Empire utterly collapsed, and all that is left of it is ruins. Yet the little baby, born in such piti-ful humility and cut down as a young man in his prime, commands the allegiance of millions of people all over the world. Although they have never seen him, he has become friend and companion to innumerable people. This undeniable fact is, by any measurement, the most astonishing phenomenon in human history. It is a solid rock of evidence that no agnostic can ever explain away.

That is why, behind all our fun and games at Christmastime, we should not try to escape a sense of awe, almost a sense of fright, at what God has done. We must never allow anything to blind us to the true significance of what happened at Bethlehem so long ago. Nothing can alter the fact that we live on a visited planet.

We shall be celebrating no beautiful myth, no lovely piece of traditional folklore, but a solemn fact. God has been here once historically, but, as millions will testify, he will come again with the same silence and the same devastating humility into any human heart ready to receive him.

Meditation

Friedrich Wilhelm Foerster

ABOVE THE PORTAL of the ancient cathedral in Lisbon is found a marvelous portrayal of the Blessed Mother with her child. Mary, the image of purity and divine grace, is not bent over the child: she is looking far, far away, as if she were contemplating the deepest meaning of the Incarnation of the divine Spirit and as if she were surveying the immeasurable consequences of the event upon which shone the star of Bethlehem. What is that deepest meaning? It becomes clear to us when we hear from the streets the cries of newspaper vendors calling out the latest news. This latest news is basically age old and constantly repeated: the cold or hot war of everyone against everyone else. Its simple cause lies in the fact that man with his intellectual gifts squanders his superiority of mind – his intelligence and passion – on animal disputes and purposes. In contrast to this, the mystery of the Incarnation brings us an eternally new, uniquely real message – a message that points to the sole fundamental solution of the problem facing all mankind: pure spirit penetrates dust-born life, leaves aside all temptation, accomplishes the whole Passion of the divine Spirit in an unspiritual world, and returns to eternity pure. But we plunge right and left into every temptation, every challenge, every folly – and the wages of sin are paid to us every time, without fail. But we will not admit that we are constantly being punished because we are constantly falling from our God-given calling; that is, because we are constantly confusing the temporal and earthly with the heavenly and the eternal.

Waiting for God

Henri Nouwen

WAITING IS NOT a very popular attitude. Waiting is not something that people think about with great sympathy. In fact, most people consider waiting a waste of time. Perhaps this is because the culture in which we live is basically saying, "Get going! Do something! Show you are able to make a difference! Don't just sit there and wait!" For many people, waiting is an awful desert between where they are and where they want to go. And people do not like such a place. They want to get out of it by doing something.

In our particular historical situation, waiting is even more difficult because we are so fearful. One of the most pervasive emotions in the atmosphere around us is fear. People are afraid – afraid of inner feelings, afraid of other people, and also afraid of the future. Fearful people have a hard time waiting, because when we are afraid we want to get away from where we are. But if we cannot flee, we may fight instead. Many of our destructive acts come from the fear that something harmful will be done to us. And if we take a broader perspective – that not only individuals but whole communities and nations might be afraid of being harmed – we can understand how hard it is to wait and how tempting it is to act. Here are the roots of a "first strike" approach to others. People who live in a world of fear are more likely to make aggressive, hostile, destructive responses than people who are not so frightened. The more afraid we are, the harder waiting becomes. That is why waiting is such an unpopular attitude for many people.

It impresses me, therefore, that all the figures who appear on the first pages of Luke's Gospel are waiting. Zechariah and Elizabeth are waiting. Mary is waiting. Simeon and Anna, who were there at the temple when Jesus was brought in, are waiting. The whole opening scene of the good news is filled with waiting people. And right at the beginning all those people in some way or another hear the words, "Do not be afraid. I have something good to say to you." These words set the tone and the context. Now Zechariah and Elizabeth, Mary, Simeon and Anna are waiting for something new and good to happen to them.

Who are these figures? They are representatives of the waiting Israel. The psalms are full of this attitude: "My soul is waiting for the Lord. I count on his word. My soul is longing for the Lord more than a watchman for daybreak. (Let the watchman count on daybreak and Israel on the Lord.) Because with the Lord there is mercy and fullness of redemption" (Psalm 130:5–7). "My soul is waiting for the Lord" – that is the song that reverberates all through the Hebrew scriptures.

But not all who dwell in Israel are waiting. In fact we might say that the prophets criticized the people (at least in part) for giving up their attentiveness to what was coming. Waiting finally became the attitude of the remnant of Israel, of that small group of Israelites that remained faithful. The prophet Zephaniah says, "In your midst I will leave a humble and lowly people, and those who are left in Israel will seek refuge in the name of Yahweh. They will do no wrong, will tell no lies; and the perjured tongue will no longer be found in their mouths" (Zephaniah 3:12–13). It is the purified remnant of faithful people who are waiting. Elizabeth and Zechariah, Mary and Simeon are representatives of that remnant. They have been able to wait, to be attentive, to live expectantly.

But what is the nature of waiting? What is the practice of waiting? How are they waiting, and how are we called to wait with them?

Waiting, as we see it in the people on the first pages of the Gospel, is waiting with a sense of promise. "Zechariah,…your wife Elizabeth is to bear you a son." "Mary,…Listen! You are to conceive and bear a son" (Luke 1:13, 31). People who wait have received a promise that allows them to wait. They have received something that is at work in them, like a seed that has started to grow. This is very important. We can only really wait if what we are waiting for has already begun for us. So waiting is never a movement from nothing to something. It is always a movement from something to something more. Zechariah,

Mary, and Elizabeth were living with a promise that nurtured them, that fed them, and that made them able to stay where they were. And in this way, the promise itself could grow in them and for them.

Second, waiting is active. Most of us think of waiting as something very passive, a hopeless state determined by events totally out of our hands. The bus is late? You cannot do anything about it, so you have to sit there and just wait. It is not difficult to understand the irritation people feel when somebody says, "Just wait." Words like that seem to push us into passivity.

But there is none of this passivity in scripture. Those who are waiting are waiting very actively. They know that what they are waiting for is growing from the ground on which they are standing. That's the secret. The secret of waiting is the faith that the seed has been planted, that something has begun. Active waiting means to be present fully to the moment, in the conviction that something is happening where you are and that you want to be present to it. A waiting person is someone who is present to the moment, who believes that this moment is *the* moment.

A waiting person is a patient person. The word *patience* means the willingness to stay where we are and live the situation out to the full in the belief that something hidden there will manifest itself to us. Impatient people are always expecting the real thing to happen somewhere else and therefore want to go elsewhere. The moment is empty. But patient people dare to stay where they are. Patient living means to live actively in the present and wait there. Waiting, then, is not passive. It involves nurturing the moment, as a mother nurtures the child that is growing in her. Zechariah, Elizabeth, and Mary were very present to the moment. That is why they could hear the angel. They were alert, attentive to the voice that spoke to them and said, "Don't be afraid. Something is happening to you. Pay attention."

But there is more. Waiting is open-ended. Open-ended waiting is hard for us because we tend to wait for something very concrete, for something that we wish to have. Much of our waiting is filled with wishes: "I wish that I would have a job. I wish that the weather would be better. I wish that the pain would go." We are full of wishes, and our waiting easily gets entangled in those wishes. For this reason, a lot of our waiting is not open-ended. Instead, our waiting is a way of controlling the future. We want the future to go in a very specific direction, and if this does not happen we are disappointed and can even slip into despair. That is why we have such a hard time waiting: we want to do the things that will make the desired events take place. Here we can see how wishes tend to be connected with fears.

But Zechariah, Elizabeth, and Mary were not filled with wishes. They were filled with hope. Hope is something very different. Hope is trusting that something will be fulfilled, but fulfilled according to the promises and not just according to our wishes. Therefore, hope is always open-ended.

I have found it very important in my own life to let go of my wishes and start hoping. It was only when I was willing to let go of wishes that something really new, something beyond my own expectations could happen to me. Just imagine what Mary was actually saying in the words, "I am the handmaid of the Lord...let what you have said be done to me" (Luke 1:38). She was saying, "I don't know what this all means, but I trust that good things will happen." She trusted so deeply that her waiting was open to all possibilities. And she did not want to control them. She believed that when she listened carefully, she could trust what was going to happen.

To wait open-endedly is an enormously radical attitude toward life. So is to trust that something will happen to us that is far beyond our own imaginings. So, too, is giving up control over our future and letting God define our life, trusting that God molds us according to God's love and not according to our fear. The spiritual life is a life in which we wait, actively present to the moment, trusting that new things will happen to us, new things that are far beyond our own imagination, fantasy, or prediction. That, indeed, is a very radical stance toward life in a world preoccupied with control.

Now let me say something about the practice of waiting. How do we wait? One of the most beautiful passages of scripture is Luke 1:39–56, which suggests that we wait together, as did Mary and Elizabeth. What happened when Mary received the words of promise? She went to Elizabeth. Something was happening to Elizabeth as well as to Mary. But how could they live that out?

I find the meeting of these two women very moving, because Elizabeth and Mary came together and enabled each other to wait. Mary's visit made Elizabeth aware of what she was waiting for. The child leapt for joy in her. Mary affirmed Elizabeth's waiting. And then Elizabeth said to Mary, "Blessed is she who believed that the promise made her by the Lord would be fulfilled." And Mary responded, "My soul proclaims the greatness of the Lord" (Luke 1:45–46). She burst into joy herself. These two women created space for each other to wait. They affirmed for each other that something was happening that was worth waiting for.

I think that is the model of the Christian community. It is a community of support, celebration, and affirmation in which we can lift up what has already begun in us. The visit of Elizabeth and Mary is one of the Bible's most beautiful expressions of what it means to form community, to be together, gathered around a promise, affirming that something is really happening.

This is what prayer is all about. It is coming together around the promise. This is what celebration is all about. It is lifting up what is already there. This is what Eucharist is about. It is saying "thank you" for the seed that has been planted. It is saying, "We are waiting for the Lord, who has already come."

The whole meaning of the Christian community lies in offering a space in which we wait for that which we have already seen. Christian community is the place where we keep the flame alive among us and take it seriously, so that it can grow and become stronger in us. In this way we can live with courage, trusting that there is a spiritual power in us that allows us to live in this world without being seduced constantly by despair, lostness, and darkness. That is how we dare to say that God is a God of love even when we see hatred all around us. That is why we can claim that God is a God of life even when we see death and destruction and agony all around us. We say it together. We affirm it in one another. Waiting together, nurturing what has already begun, expecting its fulfillment – that is the meaning of marriage, friendship, community, and the Christian life.

Our waiting is always shaped by alertness to the word. It is waiting in the knowledge that someone wants to address us. The question is, are we home? Are we at our address, ready to respond to the doorbell? We need to wait together to keep each other at home spiritually, so that when the word comes it can become flesh in us. That is why the book of God is always in the midst of those who gather. We read the word so that the word can become flesh and have a whole new life in us.

Simone Weil, a Jewish writer, said, "Waiting patiently in expectation is the foundation of the spiritual life." When Jesus speaks about the end of time, he speaks precisely about the importance of waiting. He says that nations will fight against nations and there will be wars and earthquakes and misery. People will be in agony, and they will say, "The Christ is there! No, he is here!" Everybody will be totally upset, and many will be deceived. But Jesus says you must stand ready, stay awake, stay tuned to the word of God, so that you will survive all that is going to happen and be able to stand confidently (*con-fide*, with trust) in the presence of God together in community (see Matthew 24). That is the attitude of waiting that allows us to be people who can live in a very chaotic world and survive spiritually.

In Defense of Humility

Bernard of Clairvaux

"BEHOLD," MARY SAID, "the handmaid of the Lord. Be it unto me according to your word." The virtue of humility is always found closely associated with divine grace: for God resists the proud, but gives grace to the humble (James 4:6).

Mary replies then with humility, that the dwelling of grace may be prepared. How sublime is this humility, which is incapable of yielding to the weight of honors, or of being rendered proud by them! The mother *of God* is chosen, and she declares herself his handmaid. It is in truth a mark of no ordinary humility that even when so great an honor is given her, she does not forget to be humble. It is no great thing to be humble when in a low condition;

but humility in one that is honored is a great and rare virtue.

If, for my sins or for those of others, God should permit that the Church, deceived by my pretensions, should elevate such a miserable and humble man as I to any – even the most ordinary – honor, should not I immediately, forgetful of what I am, begin to think myself such a one as men (who do not see the heart) imagine me to be? I should believe in the public opinion, not regarding the testimony of my conscience, not estimating honor by virtues, but virtue by honors; I should believe myself to be the more holy, the higher was the position I occupied. You can frequently see in the Church men sprung from the lower ranks who have attained to the higher, and who from being poor have become rich, beginning to swell with pride, forgetting their low extraction, being ashamed of their family and disdaining their parents because they are in a humble condition. You can see also wealthy men attaining rapidly to ecclesiastical honors, and then at once regarding themselves as men of great holiness, though they have changed their clothes only and not their minds.

I see (much to my regret) some who, after having despised and renounced the pomp of this world in the school of humility, habituate themselves still more to pride, and under the wings of a master who is meek and humble in heart, become more and more insolent and impatient in the cloister than they had been in the world. And what is more perverse is that many who would have had to bear contempt in their own homes cannot endure to do so in the house of God. They have not been able to obtain honors in the world, where all desire to possess them, and yet they expect to be loaded with honors, where all have made profession to despise them.

I see others (and it is a thing not to be seen without grief) who, after having enrolled themselves in the army of Christ, entangle themselves anew in the affairs of the world, and plunge again into worldly things: with earnest zeal they build up walls, but neglect to build up their own characters; under pretext of the general good, they sell their words to the rich and their salutations to matrons; but in spite of the formal order of their sovereign, they cast covetous eyes on the goods of others, and do not shrink from lawsuits to maintain their own rights. Is it so that they have crucified themselves to the world, and that the world is crucified to them, that those who before had scarcely been known in their town or village are now seen traversing provinces, frequenting courts, cultivating a knowledge of kings and the friendship of the great?

What shall I say of their religious habit itself? In it they require not so much warmth as color, and they have more care of the cleanness of their vestment than the culture of their virtues. I am ashamed to say it, but women are surpassed in their study of dress by monks, when the price of clothing is studied more than utility. These soldiers of Christ strive to be adorned, instead of arming themselves for battle. Even when they prepare for struggle, they prefer to present themselves in careful dress, and thus show themselves willing to yield without resistance – without the striking of a blow. All these evils only come when, renouncing those sentiments of humility which have caused us to leave the world, and finding ourselves thus drawn back to the unprofitable tastes and desires for worldly things, we become like dogs returning to their vomit.

Whoever we are who find such inclinations in ourselves, let us mark well what was the reply of her who was chosen to be the mother of God, but who did not forget humility. "Behold," she said, "the handmaid of the Lord; let it be to me according to your word." "Let it be to me" is the expression of desire, not the indication of doubt. These are words of prayer.

And certainly no one prays for anything unless he believes that it exists, and hopes to obtain it. But God wills that what he has promised should be asked of him in prayer. And perhaps therefore he in the first place promises many things which he has resolved to give us, that our devotion may be excited by the promise, and that thus our earnest prayer may merit what he had been disposed to bestow upon us freely. This is what the prudent Virgin understood when she joined the merit of her prayer with the previous gift of the promise freely bestowed upon her, saying, "Let it be to me according to your word." Let it be to me according to your word concerning the Word. Let the Word that was in the beginning with God become flesh from my flesh.

Let the Word, I pray, be to me, not as a word spoken only to pass away, but conceived and clothed in flesh, not in air, that he may remain with us. Let him be, not only to be heard with the ears, but to be seen with the eyes, touched with the hands and borne on the shoulders. Let the Word be to me, not as a word written and silent, but incarnate and living. That is, not traced with dead signs upon dead parchments but livingly impressed in human form upon my chaste womb; not by the tracing of a pen of lifeless reed, but by the operation of the Holy Spirit. Let it thus be to me, as was never done to anyone before me, nor after me shall be done.

I desire that he may be formed, not as the word in preaching, not as a sign in figures, or as a vision in dreams, but silently inspired, personally incarnated, found in the body, in my body. Let the Word therefore deign to do in me and for me what he needed not to do, and could not do, for himself, according to your word. Yes, let it be done for the sake of the whole world, but specially let it be done unto me, according to your word.

Annunciation

Kathleen Norris

My only rule: If I understand something, it's no mystery.
SCOTT CAIRNS

If God's incomprehensibility does not grip us in a word, if it does not draw us into his superluminous darkness, if it does not call us out of the little house of our homely, close-hugged truths…we have misunderstood the words of Christianity.
KARL RAHNER

"ANNUNCIATION" MEANS "the announcement." It would not be a scary word at all, except that as one of the Christian mysteries, it is part of a language of story, poetry, image, and symbol that the Christian tradition has employed for centuries to convey the central tenets of the faith. The Annunciation, Incarnation, Transfiguration, Resurrection. A Dominican friend defines the mysteries simply as "events in the life of Christ celebrated as stories in the gospels, and meant to be lived by believers." But modern believers tend to trust in therapy more than in mystery, a fact that tends to manifest itself in worship that employs the bland speech of pop psychology and self-help rather than language resonant with poetic meaning – for example, a call to worship that begins: "Use this hour, Lord, to get our perspectives straight again." Rather than express awe, let alone those negative feelings, fear and trembling, as we come into the presence of God, crying "Holy, Holy, Holy," we focus totally on ourselves, and arrogantly issue an imperative to God. Use this hour, because we're busy later; just send us a bill, as any therapist would, and we'll zip off a check in the mail. But the mystery of worship, which is God's presence and our response to it, does not work that way.

The profound skepticism of our age, the mistrust of all that has been handed to us by our grandfathers and grandmothers as tradition, has led to a curious failure of the imagination, manifested in language that is thoroughly comfortable, and satisfyingly unchallenging. A hymn whose name I have forgotten cheerfully asks God to "make our goals your own." A so-called prayer of confession confesses nothing but whines to God "that we have hindered your will and way for us by keeping portions of our lives apart from your influence." To my ear, such language reflects an idolatry of ourselves, that is, the notion that the measure of what we can understand, what is readily comprehensible and acceptable to us, is also the measure of God. It leads all too many clerics to simply trounce on mystery and in the process say remarkably foolish things. The Annunciation is as good as any place to start. I once heard a Protestant clergywoman say to an ecumenical assembly, "We all know there was no Virgin Birth. Mary was just an unwed, pregnant teenager, and God told her it was okay. That's the message we need to give girls today, that God loves them, and forget all this nonsense about a Virgin Birth." A gasp went up; people shook their heads. This was the first (and only) gratuitously offensive remark made at a convention marked by great theological diversity. When it came, I happened to be sitting between some Russian Orthodox, who were offended theologically, and black

Baptists, whose sense of theological affront was mixed with social concern. They were not at all pleased to hear a well-educated, middle-class white woman say that what we need to tell pregnant teenagers is, "It's okay."

I realized that my own anger at the woman's arrogance had deep personal roots. I was taken back to my teenage years, when the "de-mythologizing" of Christianity that I had encountered in a misguided study of modern theology had led me to conclude that there was little in religion for me. In the classroom, at least, it seemed that anything in the Bible that didn't stand up to reason, that we couldn't explain, was primitive, infantile, ripe for discarding. So I took all my longing for the sacred, for mystery, into the realm of poetry, and found a place for myself there. Now, more than thirty years later, I sat in a room full of Christians and thought, *My God, they're still at it, still trying to leach every bit of mystery out of this religion, still substituting the most trite language imaginable. You're okay, the boy you screwed when you were both too drunk to stand is okay, all God chooses to say about it is, it's okay.*

The job of any preacher, it seems to me, is not to dismiss the Annunciation because it doesn't appeal to modern prejudices but to remind congregations of why it might still be an important story. I once heard a Benedictine friend who is an Assiniboine Indian preach on the Annunciation to an Indian congregation. "The first thing Gabriel does when he encounters Mary," he said, "is to give her a new name: 'Most favored one.' It's a naming ceremony," he emphasized, making a connection that excited and delighted his listeners. When I brood on the story of the Annunciation, I like to think about what it means to be "overshadowed" by the Holy Spirit; I wonder if a kind of overshadowing isn't what every young woman pregnant for the first time might feel, caught up in something so much larger than herself. I think of James Wright's little poem "Trouble," and the wonder of his pregnant mill-town girl. The butt of jokes, the taunt of gossips, she is amazed to carry such power within herself. "Sixteen years, and / all that time, she thought she was nothing / but skin and bones." Wright's poem does, it seems to me, what the clergywoman talks about doing, but without resorting to ideology or the false assurance that "it's okay." Told all her life that she is "nothing," the girl discovers in herself another, deeper reality. A mystery; something holy, with a potential for salvation. The poem has challenged me for years to wonder what such a radically new sense of oneself would entail. Could it be a form of virgin birth?

Wondering at the many things that the story of the Annunciation might mean, I take refuge in the fact that for centuries so many poets and painters have found it worthy of consideration. European art would not have been enriched had Fra Angelico, or Dante Gabriel Rossetti for that matter, simply realized that the Annunciation was a form of negative thinking, moralistic nonsense that only a modern mindset – resolutely intellectual, professional, therapeutic – could have straightened out for them. I am glad also that many artists and poets are still willing to explore the metaphor (and by that I mean the truth) of the Virgin Birth. The contemporary poet Laurie Sheck, in her poem "The Annunciation," respects the "honest grace" that Mary shows by not attempting to hide her fear in the presence of the angel, her fear of the changes within her body. I suspect that Mary's "yes" to her new identity, to the immense and wondrous possibilities of her new and holy name, may provide an excellent means of conveying to girls that there is something in them that no man can touch; that belongs only to them, and to God.

When I hear remarks like the one made by the pastor at that conference, I am struck mainly by how narrow and impoverished a concept of virginity it reveals. It's in the monastic world that I find a broader and also more relevant grasp of what it could mean to be virgin. Thomas Merton, in *Conjectures of a Guilty Bystander*, describes the true identity that he seeks in contemplative prayer as a "point vierge" at the center of his being, "a point untouched by illusion, a point of pure truth…which belongs entirely to God, which is inaccessible to the fantasies of our own mind or the brutalities of our own will. This little point…of absolute poverty," he wrote, "is the pure glory of God in us."

It is only when we stop idolizing the illusion of our control over the events of life and recognize our poverty that we become virgin in the sense that Merton means. Adolescents tend to be better at this than grown-ups, because they are continually told that they don't know enough, and they lack the means to hide behind professional credentials. The whole world confirms to them that they are indeed poor, regrettably laboring through what is called "the awkward age." It is no wonder that teenagers like to run in packs, that they surround themselves with people as gawky and unformed as themselves. But it is in adolescence that the fully formed adult self begins to emerge, and if a person has been fortunate, allowed to develop at his or her own pace, this self is a liberating force, and it is virgin. That is, it is one-in-itself, better able to cope with peer pressure, as it can more readily measure what is true to one's self, and what would violate it. Even adolescent self-absorption recedes as one's capacity for the mystery of hospitality grows: it is only as one is at home in oneself that one may be truly hospitable to others – welcoming, but not overbearing, affably pliant but not subject to crass manipulation. This difficult balance is maintained only as one remains virgin, cognizant of oneself as valuable, unique, and undiminishable at core...

We all need to be told that God loves us, and the mystery of the Annunciation reveals an aspect of that love. But it also suggests that our response to this love is critical. A few verses before the angel appears to

Mary in the first chapter of Luke's Gospel, another annunciation occurs; an angel announces to an old man, Zechariah, that his equally aged wife is to bear a son who will "make ready a people prepared for the Lord." The couple are to name him John; he is known to us as John the Baptist. Zechariah says to the angel, "How will I know that this is so?" which is a radically different response from the one Mary makes. She says, "How can this be?"

I interpret this to mean that while Zechariah is seeking knowledge and information, Mary contents herself with wisdom, with pondering a state of being. God's response to Zechariah is to strike him dumb during the entire term of his son's gestation, giving him a pregnancy of his own. He does not speak again until after the child is born, and he has written on a tablet what the angel has said to him: "His name is John." This confounds his relatives, who had expected that the child would be named after his father. I read Zechariah's punishment as a grace, in that he could not say anything to further compound his initial arrogance when confronted with mystery. When he does speak again, it is to praise God; he's had nine months to think it over.

Mary's "How can this be?" is a simpler response than Zechariah's, and also more profound. She does not lose her voice but finds it. Like any of the prophets, she asserts herself before God saying, "Here am I." There is no arrogance, however, but only holy fear and wonder. Mary proceeds – as we must do in life – making her commitment without knowing much about what it will entail or where it will lead. I treasure the story because it forces me to ask: When the mystery of God's love breaks through into my consciousness, do I run from it? Do I ask of it what it cannot answer? Shrugging, do I retreat into facile clichés, the popular but false wisdom of what "we all know"? Or am I virgin enough to respond from my deepest, truest self, and say something new, a "yes" that will change me forever?

Where God Enters

Meister Eckhart

For while all things were in quiet silence and the night was in the midst of her course...

WISDOM OF SOLOMON 18:14–15

HERE IN TIME WE MAKE HOLIDAY because the eternal birth which God the father bore and bears unceasingly in eternity is now born in time, in human nature. Saint Augustine says this birth is always happening. But if it does not happen in me, what does it profit me? What matters is that it shall happen in me.

We intend therefore to speak of this birth as taking place in us, as being consummated in the virtuous soul, for it is in the perfect soul that God speaks his word. What I shall say is true only of the devout man, of him who has walked and is still walking in the way of God, not of the natural undisciplined man who is entirely remote from and unconscious of this birth.

There is a saying of the wise man, "When all things lay in the midst of silence, then leapt there down into me from on high, from the royal throne, a secret word." This sermon is about this word.

Concerning it three things are to be noted. The first is where in the soul God the father speaks his Word, where she is receptive of this act, where this birth occurs. The second, has to do with man's conduct in relation to this act, this interior speaking, this birth. The third point will deal with the profit, and how great it is, that accrues from this birth.

Note in the first place that in what I am about to say I intend to use natural proofs that you yourselves can grasp, for though I put more faith in the scriptures than myself, nevertheless it is easier and better for you to learn by arguments that can be verified.

First we will take the words, "In the midst of the silence there was spoken in me a secret word." But, sir, where is the silence and where the place in which the word is spoken?

To begin with, it is spoken in the purest, noblest ground, yes, in the very center of the soul. That is mid-silence, for no creature ever entered there, nor any image, nor has the soul there either activity or understanding, therefore she is not aware of any image either of herself or any creature. Whatever the soul effects, she effects with her powers. When she understands, she understands with her intellect. When she remembers, she does so with her memory. When she loves, she does so with her will. She works then with her powers and not with her essence.

Now every exterior act is linked with some means. The power of seeing is brought into play only through the eyes; elsewhere she can neither do nor bestow such a thing as seeing. And so with all the other senses; their operations are always effected through some means or other. But there is no activity in the essence of the soul; the faculties she works with emanate from the ground of the essence, but in her actual ground there is mid-silence; here alone is a rest and habitation for this birth, this act, wherein God the father speaks his word, for she is intrinsically receptive of nothing but the divine essence, without means. Here God enters the soul with his all, not merely with a part. God enters the ground of the soul.

None can touch the ground of the soul but God. No creature is admitted into her ground, it must stop outside in her powers. There it sees the image whereby it has been drawn in and found shelter. For when the soul's powers contact a creature, they set out to make of the creature an image and likeness which they absorb. By it they know the creature. Creatures cannot enter the soul, nor can the soul know anything about a creature whose image she has not willingly taken into herself. She approaches creatures through their present images, an image being a thing that the soul creates with her powers. Be it a stone, a rose, a person, or anything else she wants to know about, she gets out the image of it which she has already taken in and thus is able to unite herself with it. But an image received in this way must of necessity enter from without through the senses. Consequently, there is nothing so unknown to the soul as herself. The soul, says the philosopher, can neither create nor absorb an image of herself. So she has nothing to know herself by. Images all enter through the senses, hence she can have no image of herself. She knows other things but not herself. Of nothing does she know so little as herself, owing to this arrangement.

Now you must know that inwardly the soul is free from means and images; that is why God can freely unite with her without form or image. You cannot but attribute to God without measure whatever power you attribute to a master. The wiser and more powerful the master, the more immediately is his work effected and the simpler it is. Man requires many instruments for his external works; much preparation is needed before he can bring them forth as he has imagined them. The sun and moon, whose work is to give light, in their mastership perform this very swiftly: the instant their radiance is poured forth, all the ends of the earth are filled with light. More exalted are the angels, who need fewer means for their works and have fewer images. The highest Seraph has but a single image. He seizes as a unity all that his inferiors regard as manifold. Now God needs no image and has no image: without image, likeness, or means does God work in the soul, in her ground wherein no image ever entered other than himself with his own essence. This no creature can do.

How does God the father give birth to his son in the soul? Like creatures, in image and likeness? No, by my faith, but just as he gives him birth in eternity and not otherwise.

Well, but how does he give him birth there?

See, God the father has perfect insight into himself, profound and thorough knowledge of himself by means of himself, not by means of any image. And thus God the father gives birth to his son in the very oneness of the divine nature. Thus it is, and in no other way, that God the father gives birth to his son in the ground and essence of the soul, and thus he unites himself with her. Were any image present, there would be no real union, and in real union lies true bliss.

Now you may say: "But there is nothing innate in the soul but images." No, not so! If that were true, the soul would never be happy, but God made every creature to enjoy perfect happiness, otherwise God would not be the highest happiness and final goal, whereas it is his will and nature to be the alpha and omega of all. No creature can be happiness. And here indeed can just as little be perfection, for perfection (perfect virtue, that is to say) results from perfection of life. Therefore you truly must sojourn and dwell in your essence, in your ground, and there God shall mix you with his essence without the medium of any image. No image represents and signifies itself: it stands for that of which it is the image. Now seeing that you have no image other than what is outside you, therefore it is impossible for you to be beatified by any image whatsoever.

The second point is, what must a person do to deserve and procure this birth that it may come to pass and be consummated in him? Is it better for him to do his part toward it, to imagine and think about God, or should he keep still in peace and quiet so that God can act in him while he merely waits on God's operation? Of course, I am referring to those whose act is only for the good and perfect, those who have so absorbed and assimilated the essence of virtue that it emanates from them naturally, without their seeking. They live a worthy life and have within them the lofty teaching of our Lord Jesus Christ. Such are permitted to know that the very best and utmost of attainment in this life is to remain still and let God act and speak in you. When the powers have all been withdrawn from their bodily forms and functions, then this word is spoken. Thus he says: "In the midst of the silence the secret word was spoken to me."

The more completely you are able to draw in your faculties and forget those things and their images which you have taken in – the more, that is to say, you forget the creature – the nearer you are to this and the more susceptible you are to it. If only you could suddenly be altogether unaware of things, could you but pass into oblivion of your own existence as Saint Paul did when he said: "Whether in the body I know not, or out of the body I know not, God knows!" Here the Spirit had so entirely absorbed the faculties that it had forgotten the body: memory no longer functioned, nor understanding, nor the senses, nor even those powers whose duty it is to govern and grace the body; vital warmth and energy were arrested so that the body remained intact throughout the three days during which he neither ate nor drank. It was the same with Moses when he fasted forty days on the mount and was none the worse for it: on the last day he was as strong as on the first.

Thus a person must abscond from his senses, invert his faculties, and lapse into oblivion of things and of himself. About which the philosopher addressed the soul: "Withdraw from the restlessness of external activities!" And again: "Flee away and hide from the turmoil of outward occupations and inward thoughts, for they create nothing but discord!" If God is to speak his word in the soul, she must be at rest and at peace; then he speaks in his soul his word and *himself:* not an image but himself. Dionysius says: "God has no image or likeness of himself, seeing that he is intrinsically all good, truth and being." God performs all his works in himself and outside himself simultaneously. Do not fondly imagine that God, when he created the heavens and the earth and all creatures, made one thing one day and another the next.

All God did was: he willed and they were. God works without instrument and without image. And the freer you are from images, the more receptive you are to his interior operation, and the more introverted and oblivious you are, the closer you are to it. All things must be forsaken. God scorns to work among images.

Now you may say, "What is it that God does without images in the ground and essence?" That I am incapable of knowing, for my soul powers can receive only in images; they have to recognize and lay hold of each thing in its appropriate image: they cannot recognize a bird in the image of a man. Now since images all enter from without, this is concealed from my soul, which is most salutary for her. Not knowing makes her wonder and leads her to eager pursuit, for she knows clearly *that* it is but knows not *how* nor *what* it is. No sooner does one know the reason of a thing than he tires of it and goes casting about for something new. Always clamoring to know, we are ever inconstant. The soul is constant only to this unknowing which keeps her pursuing.

The wise man said concerning this: "In the middle of the night when all things were in quiet silence, there was spoken to me a hidden word." It came like a thief, by stealth. What does he mean by a word that was hidden? The nature of a word is to reveal what is hidden. It appeared before me, shining out with intent to reveal and giving me knowledge of God. Hence it is called a word. But what it was remained hidden from me. That was its stealthy coming "in a whispering stillness to reveal itself." It is just because it is hidden that one is always and must be always after it. It appears and disappears; we are meant to yearn and sigh for it.

Saint Paul says we ought to pursue this until we spy it and not stop until we grasp it. When he returned after being caught up into the third heaven, where God was made known to him and where he beheld all things, he had forgotten nothing, but it was so deep down in his ground that his intellect could not reach it; it was veiled from him. He was therefore obliged to pursue it and search for it in himself, not outside himself. It is not outside, it is inside: wholly within. And being convinced of this, he said: "I am sure that neither death nor any affliction can separate me from what I find within me."

There is a fine saying of one philosopher to another about this. He says: "I am aware of something in me which sparkles in my intelligence; I clearly perceive *that* it is something, but *what* I cannot grasp. Yet it seems if I could only seize it I should know its truth." To which the other philosopher replied, "Follow it boldly! For if you can seize it, you will possess the sum total of all good and have eternal life!" It hides yet it shows. It comes, but after the manner of a thief, with intent to take and to steal all things from the soul. By emerging and showing itself somewhat, it purposes to decoy the soul and to draw it to itself, to rob it and take itself from it. As the prophet said: "Lord take from them their spirit and give them instead thy spirit." This too the loving soul meant when she said, "My soul dissolved and melted away when Love spoke his word; when he entered I could not but fail." And Christ signified it by his words: "Whosoever shall leave anything for my sake shall be paid an hundredfold, and whosoever will possess me must deny himself and all things, and whosoever will serve me must follow me nor go anymore after his own."

Those who have written of the soul's nobility have gone no further than their natural intelligence could carry them: they never entered her ground, so that much remained obscure and unknown to them. "I will sit in silence and hearken to what God speaks within me," said the prophet. Into this retirement steals the word in the darkness of the night. Saint John says, "The light shines in the darkness; it came unto its own and as many as received it became in authority sons of God: to them was given power to become God's sons."

Notice the fruit and use of this mysterious word and of this darkness. In this gloom which is his own, the heavenly father's son is not born alone: you too are born there a child of the same heavenly father and no other, and to you also he gives power. Call this if you will an ignorance, an unknowing, yet there is in it more than all knowing and understanding without it, for this outward ignorance lures and attracts you from all understood things and from yourself. This is what Christ meant when he said, "Whosoever denies not himself and leaves not father and mother and is not estranged from all these, he is not worthy of me." As though to say: he who abandons not creaturely externals can neither be conceived nor born in this divine birth. But divesting yourself of yourself and of everything external does indeed give it to you.

May the God who has been born again as man assist us in this birth, continually helping us, weak men, to be born again in him as God. Amen.

The Divine Dawning

Karl Rahner

Light of lights! All gloom dispelling,
Thou didst come to make thy dwelling
Here within our world of sight.
Lord, in pity and in power,
Thou didst in our darkest hour
Rend the clouds and show thy light.

Praise to thee in earth and heaven
Now and evermore be given,
Christ, who art our sun and shield.
Lord, for us thy life thou gavest,
Those who trust in thee thou savest,
All thy mercy stands revealed.

ST. THOMAS AQUINAS

EVERY YEAR WE CELEBRATE the holy season of Advent, O God. Every year we pray those beautiful prayers of longing and waiting, and sing those lovely songs of hope and promise. Every year we roll up all our needs and yearnings and faithful expectation into one word: "Come!"

And yet, what a strange prayer this is! After all, you have already come and pitched your tent among us. You have already shared our life with its little joys, its long days of tedious routine, its bitter end. Could we invite you to anything more than this with our "Come"? Could you approach any nearer to us than you did when you became the "Son of Man," when you adopted our ordinary little ways so thoroughly that it's almost hard for us to distinguish you from the rest of our fellow men?

In spite of all this we still pray: "Come." And this word issues as much from the depth of our hearts as it did long ago from the hearts of our forefathers, the kings and prophets who saw your day still far off in the distance, and fervently blessed its coming. Is it true, then, that we only "celebrate" this season, or is it still really Advent?

Are you the eternal Advent? Are you he who is always still to come, but never arrives in such a way as to fulfill our expectations? Are you the infinitely distant One, who can never be reached?

Are you only the distant horizon surrounding the world of our deeds and sufferings, the horizon which, no matter where we roam, is always just as far away? Are you only the eternal Today, containing within itself all time and all change, equally near to everything, and thus also equally distant?

When our bleeding feet have apparently covered a part of the distance to your eternity, don't you always retreat twice as far away from us, into the immense reaches filled only by your infinite being? Has humanity drawn the least bit closer to you in the thousands and thousands of years that have elapsed since it boldly began its most exciting and fearsome adventure, the search for you?

Have I come any nearer to you in the course of my life, or doesn't all the ground I have won only make my cup all the more bitter because the distance to you is still infinite? Must we remain ever far from you, O God of immensity, because you are ever near to us, and therefore have no need of "coming" to us? Is it because there is no place in our world to which you must first "find your way"?

You tell me that you have really already come, that your name is Jesus, Son of Mary, and that I know in what place and at what time I can find you. That's all true, of course, Lord – but forgive me if I say that this coming of yours seems to me more like a going, more like a departure than an arrival.

You have clothed yourself in the form of a slave. You, the hidden God, have been found as one of us. You have quietly and inconspicuously taken your place in our ranks and marched along with us. You have walked with us, even though we are beings who are never coming, but rather always going, since any goal we reach has only one purpose: to point beyond itself and lead us to the last goal, our end.

And thus we still cry: "Come! Come to us, you who never pass away, you whose day has no evening, whose reality knows no end! Come to us, because our march is only a procession to the grave." Despairing of ourselves, we call upon you – *then* most of all, when, in composure and quiet resignation, we bring ourselves to accept our finiteness.

You promised that you would come, and actually made good your promise. But how, O Lord, how did you come? You did it by taking a human life as your own. You became like us in everything: born of a woman, you suffered under Pontius Pilate, were crucified, died, and were buried. And thus you took up again the very thing we wanted to discard. You began what we thought would end with your coming: our poor human kind of life, which is sheer frailty, finiteness, and death.

Contrary to all our fond hopes, you seized upon precisely this kind of human life and made it your own. And you did this not in order to change or abolish it, not so that you could visibly and tangibly transform it, not to divinize it. You didn't even fill it to overflowing with the kind of goods that men are able to wrest from the small, rocky acre of their temporal life, and which they laboriously store away as their meager provision for eternity.

No, you took upon yourself our kind of life, just as it is. You let it slip away from you, just as ours vanishes from us. You held on to it carefully, so that not a single drop of its torments would be spilled. You hoarded its every fleeting moment, so you could suffer through it all, right to the bitter end.

You too felt the inexorable wheel of blind, brute nature rolling over your life, while the clear-seeing eye of human malice looked on in cruel satisfaction. And when your humanity glanced upwards to the One who, in purest truth and deepest love, is called "Father," it too caught sight of the God whose ways are unfathomable and whose judgments are incomprehensible, who hands us the chalice or lets it pass, all according to his own holy will. You too learned in the hard school of suffering that no "why" will ever ferret out the secret of that will, which could have done otherwise, and yet chose to do something we would never understand.

You were supposed to come to redeem us from ourselves, and yet you, who alone are absolutely free and unbounded, were "made," even as we are. Of course, I know that you remained what you always were, but still, didn't our mortality make you shudder, you the Immortal God? Didn't you, the broad and limitless Being, shrink back in horror from our narrowness? Weren't you, absolute Truth, revolted at our pretense?

Didn't you nail yourself to the cross of creation, when you took as your own life something which you had drawn out of nothing, when you assumed as your very own the darkness that you had previously spread out in the eternal distance as the background to your own inaccessible light? Isn't the Cross of Golgotha only the visible form of the cross you have prepared for yourself, which towers throughout the spaces of eternity?

Is *that* your real coming? Is that what humanity has been waiting for? Is that why men have made the whole of human history a single great Advent-choir, in which even the blasphemers take part – a single chant crying out for you and your coming? Is your humble human existence from Bethlehem to Calvary really the coming that was to redeem wretched humanity from its misery?

Is our grief taken from us, simply because you wept too? Is our surrender to finiteness no longer a terrible act of despair, simply because you also capitulated? Does our road, which doesn't want to end, have a happy ending despite itself, just because you are traveling it with us?

But how can this be? And why should it be? How can our life be the redemption of itself, simply because it has also become your life? How can you buy us back from the law, simply by having fallen under the law yourself (Gal. 4:5)?

Or is it this way: is my surrender to the crushing narrowness of earthly existence the beginning of my liberation from it, precisely because this surrender is my "Amen" to your human life, my way of saying yes to your human coming, which happens in a manner so contrary to my expectations?

But of what value is it to me that my destiny is now a participation in yours, if you have merely made what is mine your own? Or have you made my life only the *beginning* of your coming, only the starting point of your life?

Slowly a light is beginning to dawn. I've begun to understand something I have known for a long time: You are still in the process of your coming. Your appearance in the form of a slave was only the beginning of your coming, a beginning in which you chose to redeem men by embracing the very slavery from which you were freeing them. And *you* can really achieve your purpose in this paradoxical way, because the paths that *you* tread have a real ending, the narrow passes which *you* enter soon open out into broad liberty, the cross that *you* carry inevitably becomes a brilliant banner of triumph.

It is said that you will come again, and this is true. But the word *again* is misleading. It won't really be "another" coming, because you have never really gone away. In the human existence that you made your own for all eternity, you have never left us.

But still you will come again, because the fact that you have already come must continue to be revealed ever more clearly. It will become progressively more manifest to the world that the heart of all things is already transformed, because you have taken them all to your heart.

Behold, you come. And your coming is neither past nor future, but the present, which has only to reach its fulfillment. Now it is still the one single hour of your Advent, at the end of which we too shall have found out that you have really come.

O God who is to come, grant me the grace to live now, in the hour of your Advent, in such a way that I may merit to live in you forever, in the blissful hour of your eternity.

Concerning the Light

Isaac Penington

In him was life, and the life was the light of men. And the light shineth in darkness, and the darkness comprehendeth it not.

JOHN 1: 4–5

WHAT IS THE DARKNESS which comprehendeth not the light? Is it not man in the unregenerate state? "Ye were darkness," saith the apostle, speaking concerning them as they had been in that state.

Now it pleaseth the Lord, that in this darkness his pure light should shine, to gather man out of the darkness. For unless light should shine on man in his dark state, he could never be gathered out of it; but he that is turned to the light, and followeth it, cannot abide in the darkness; but cometh into that which gathereth and preserveth the mind out of it.

But of what nature is this light, which shineth in man in his dark state? It is of a living nature; it is light which flows from life; it is light which hath life in it; it is the life of our Lord Jesus Christ, of the Word eternal, which is the light of men. And he who cometh to the true understanding, may thereby distinguish it from all other lights whatsoever.

There is a vast difference between it, and the reason and understanding of a man; for the natural man, with his understanding, is dead; but this is living, and powerfully operating in man, as it finds entrance, and as his mind is joined to it. He that is dead, indeed, knows it not; but he that is alive unto God, feels the virtue of it. This light is above all gathered knowledge, and above all descriptions whatsoever, for it is of the nature of Him from whom it flows.

A man may get a notion from this into his mind, which he may retain the knowledge of; but his knowledge will quickly die. But he that dwells in the light… dwells in that which never dies.

A Sky Full of Children

Madeleine L'Engle

I WALK OUT ONTO THE DECK of my cottage, looking up at the great river of the Milky Way flowing across the sky. A sliver of a moon hangs in the southwest, with the evening star gently in the curve.

Evening. Evening of this day. Evening of my own life.

I look at the stars and wonder. How old is the universe? All kinds of estimates have been made and, as far as we can tell, not one is accurate. All we know is that once upon a time or, rather, once before time, Christ called everything into being in a great breath of creativity – waters, land, green growing things, birds and beasts, and finally human creatures – the beginning, the genesis, not in ordinary Earth days;

the Bible makes it quite clear that God's time is different from our time. A thousand years for us is no more than the blink of an eye to God. But in God's good time the universe came into being, opening up from a tiny flower of nothingness to great clouds of hydrogen gas to swirling galaxies. In God's good time came solar systems and planets and ultimately this planet on which I stand on this autumn evening as the Earth makes its graceful dance around the sun. It takes one Earth day, one Earth night, to make a full turn, part of the intricate pattern of the universe. And God called it good, very good.

A sky full of God's children! Each galaxy, each star, each living creature, every particle and subatomic particle of creation, we are all children of the Maker. From a subatomic particle with a life span of a few seconds, to a galaxy with a life span of billions of years, to us human creatures somewhere in the middle in size and age, we are made in God's image, male and female, and we are, as Christ promised us, God's children by adoption and grace.

Children of God, made in God's image. How? Genesis gives no explanations, but we do know instinctively that it is not a physical image. God's explanation is to send Jesus, the incarnate One, God enfleshed. Don't try to explain the Incarnation to me! It is further from being explainable than the furthest star in the furthest galaxy. It is love, God's limitless love enfleshing that love into the form of a human being, Jesus, the Christ, fully human and fully divine.

Was there a moment, known only to God, when all the stars held their breath, when the galaxies paused in their dance for a fraction of a second, and the Word, who had called it all into being, went with all his love into the womb of a young girl, and the universe started to breathe again, and the ancient harmonies resumed their song, and the angels clapped their hands for joy?

Power. Greater power than we can imagine, abandoned, as the Word knew the powerlessness of the unborn child, still unformed, taking up almost no space in the great ocean of amniotic fluid, unseeing, unhearing, unknowing. Slowly growing, as any human embryo grows, arms and legs and a head, eyes, mouth, nose, slowly swimming into life until the ocean in the womb is no longer large enough, and it is time for birth.

Christ, the Second Person of the Trinity, Christ, the Maker of the universe or perhaps many universes, willingly and lovingly leaving all that power and coming to this poor, sin-filled planet to live with us for a few years to show us what we ought to be and could be. Christ came to us as Jesus of Nazareth, wholly human and wholly divine, to show us what it means to be made in God's image.

Jesus, as Paul reminds us, was the firstborn of many brethren.

I stand on the deck of my cottage, looking at the sky full of God's children, and know that I am one of them.

The Shaking Reality
of Advent

Alfred Delp

Condemned as a traitor for his opposition to Hitler, Father Alfred Delp, a Jesuit priest, wrote this piece in a Nazi prison shortly before he was hanged in 1945.

THERE IS PERHAPS NOTHING we modern people need more than to be genuinely shaken up. Where life is firm we need to sense its firmness; and where it is unstable and uncertain and has no basis, no foundation, we need to know this too and endure it.

We may ask why God has sent us into this time, why he has sent this whirlwind over the earth, why he keeps us in this chaos where all appears hopeless and dark and why there seems to be no end to this in sight. The answer to this question is perhaps that we were living on earth in an utterly false and counterfeit security. And now God strikes the earth till it resounds, now he shakes and shatters; not to pound us with fear, but to teach us one thing – the spirit's innermost moving and being moved.

Many of the things that are happening today would never have happened if we had been living in that movement and disquiet of heart which results when we are faced with God, the Lord, and when we look clearly at things as they really are. If we had done this, God would have withheld his hand from many things that have stirred up and shaken and crushed our lives. We would have seen the inner authorities, we would have seen and judged the limits of our own competence.

But we have stood on this earth in false pathos, in false security; in our spiritual insanity we really believed we could, with the power of our own hand and arm, bring the stars down from heaven and kindle flames of eternity in the world. We believed that with our own forces we could avert the dangers and banish night, switch off and halt the internal quaking of the universe. We believed we could harness every-thing and fit it into a final order that would stand.

Here is the message of Advent: faced with him who is the Last, the world will begin to shake. Only when we do not cling to false securities will our eyes be able to see this Last One and get to the bottom of things. Only then will we be able to guard our life from the frights and terrors into which God the Lord has let the world sink to teach us, so that we may awaken from sleep, as Paul says, and see that it is time to repent, time to change things. It is time to say, "All right, it was night; but let that be over now and let us be ready for the day." We must do this with a decision that comes out of these very horrors we have experienced and all that is connected with them; and because of this our decision will be unshakable even in uncertainty.

If we want to transform life again, if Advent is truly to come again – the Advent of home and of hearts, the Advent of the people and the nations, a coming of the Lord in all this – then the great Advent ques-tion for us is whether we come out of these convul-sions with this determination: yes, arise! It is time to awaken from sleep. It is time for a waking up to begin somewhere. It is time to put things back where God the Lord put them. It is time for each of us to go to work, with the same unshakable sureness that the Lord will come, to set our life in God's order wherever we can. Where God's word is heard, he will not cheat our life of the message; where our life rebels before our own eyes he will reprimand it.

The world today needs people who have been shaken by ultimate calamities and emerged from them with the knowledge and awareness that those who look to the Lord will still be preserved by him, even if they are hounded from the earth.

The Advent message comes out of an encounter of man with the absolute, the final, the gospel. It is thus the message that shakes – so that in the end the world shall be shaken. The fact that then the Son of man shall come is more than a historic prophecy; it is also a decree, that God's coming and the shaking up of humanity are somehow connected. If we are inwardly unshaken, inwardly incapable of being genuinely shaken, if we become obstinate and hard and superficial and cheap, then God will himself intervene in world events and teach us what it means to be placed in this agitation and be stirred inwardly.

Then the great question to us is whether we are still capable of being truly shocked or whether it is to remain so that we see thousands of things and know that they should not be and must not be, and that we get hardened to them. How many things have we become used to in the course of the years, of the weeks and months, so that we stand unshocked , unstirred, inwardly unmoved.

Advent is a time when we ought to be shaken and brought to a realization of ourselves. The necessary condition for the fulfillment of Advent is the renunciation of the presumptuous attitudes and alluring dreams in which and by means of which we always build ourselves imaginary worlds. In this way we force reality to take us to itself by force – by force, in much pain and suffering.

This shocked awakening is definitely part of experiencing Advent. But at the same time there is much more that belongs to it. Advent is blessed with God's promises, which constitute the hidden happiness of this time. These promises kindle the inner light in our hearts. Being shattered, being awakened – only with these is life made capable of Advent. In the bitterness of awakening, in the helplessness of "coming to," in the wretchedness of realizing our limitations, the golden threads that pass between heaven and earth in these times reach us. These golden threads give the world a taste of the abundance it can have.

We must not shy away from Advent thoughts of this kind. We must let our inner eye see and let our hearts range far. We will encounter the earnestness of Advent and the blessing of Advent in a different way. We will see characters, completed and whole personalities, that belong to these days and to all days – characters in whom the Advent message and the Advent blessing simply exist and live, calling out to us and touching us to cheer and shake us, to console and to uplift us.

I am referring to characters that live in these days and all days. The types I mean are these three: the Angel of Annunciation, the Blessed Woman, and the Crier in the Wilderness.

The Angel of Annunciation. I see Advent this year with greater intensity and anticipation than ever before. Walking up and down in my cell, three paces this way and three paces that way, with my hands in irons and ahead of me an uncertain fate, I have a new and different understanding of God's promise of redemption and release.

This reminds me of the angel that was given to me two years ago for Advent by a kind person. The angel bore the inscription, "Rejoice, for the Lord is near." The angel was destroyed by a bomb. A bomb killed the man who gave it to me, and I often feel he is doing me the service of an angel.

The horror of these times would be unendurable unless we kept being cheered and set upright again by the promises that are spoken. The angels of annunciation, speaking their message of blessing into the midst of anguish, scattering their seed of blessing that will one day spring up amid the night, call us to hope. These are not yet the loud angels of rejoicing and fulfillment that come out into the open, the angels of Advent. Quiet, inconspicuous, they come into rooms and before hearts as they did then. Quietly they bring God's questions and proclaim to us the wonders of God, for whom nothing is impossible.

For all its earnestness, Advent is a time of inner security, because it has received a message. Oh, if it ever happens that we forget the message and the promises; if all we know is the four walls and the prison windows of our gray days; if we can no longer hear the gentle step of the announcing angels; if our soul no longer is at once shaken and exalted by their whispered word – then it will be all over with us. We are living wasted time and are dead before they do us any harm.

The first thing we must do if we want to be alive is to believe in the golden seed of God that the angels have scattered and still offer to open hearts. The second thing is to walk through these gray days oneself as an announcing messenger. So many need their courage strengthened, so many are in despair and in need of consolation, there is so much harshness that needs a gentle hand and an illuminating word, so much loneliness crying out for a word of release, so much loss and pain in search of inner meaning. God's messengers know of the blessing that the Lord has cast like seed into these hours of history. Understanding this world in the light of Advent means to endure in faith, waiting for the fertility of the silent earth, the abundance of the coming harvest. Not because we put our trust in the earth but because we have heard God's message and have met one of God's announcing angels ourselves.

The Blessed Woman. She is the most comforting of all the Advent figures. Advent's holiest consolation is that the angel's annunciation met with a ready heart. The Word became flesh in a motherly heart and grew out far beyond itself into the world of God-humanity. What good does it do us to sense and feel our misery unless a bridge is thrown over to the other shore? What help is it to be terrified at our lostness and confusion unless a light flashes up that is a match for darkness and always is its master? What good does it do to shiver in the coldness and hardness in which the world freezes as it goes deeper astray in itself and kills itself, unless we also come to know of the grace that is mightier than the peril of oblivion?

Poets and myth-makers and mankind's other tellers of stories and fairy tales have often spoken of mothers. One time they meant the earth; another time they meant nature. By this word they tried to disclose the mysterious creative fount of all things, to conjure up the welling mystery of life. In all this there was hunger and anticipation and longing and Advent – waiting for this blessed woman.

That God became a mother's son; that there could be a woman walking the earth whose womb was consecrated to be the holy temple and tabernacle of God – that is actually earth's perfection and the fulfillment of its expectations.

So many kinds of Advent consolation stream from the mysterious figure of the blessed, expectant Mary. The gray horizons must grow light. It is only the immediate scene that shouts so loudly and insistently. Beyond these things is a different realm, one that is now in our midst. The woman has conceived the child, sheltered it beneath her heart, and given birth to the Son. The world has come under a different law. We are not speaking of only historical events that happened once, on which our salvation rests. Advent is the promise denoting the new order of things, of life, of our existence.

We must remember today with courage that the blessed woman of Nazareth foreshadows the light in our midst today. Deeper down in our being, our days and our destinies, too, bear the blessing and mystery of God. The blessed woman waits, and we must wait too until her hour has come.

The One Who Cries in the Wilderness. Woe to an age when the voices of those who cry in the wilderness have fallen silent, outshouted by the noise of the day or outlawed or swallowed up in the intoxication of progress, or growing smothered and fainter for fear and cowardice. The devastation will soon be so terrifying and universal that the word "wilderness" will again strike our hearts and minds. I think we know that.

But still there are no crying voices to raise their plaint and accusation. Not for an hour can life dispense with these John-the-Baptist characters, these original individuals, struck by the lightning of mission and vocation. Their heart goes before them, and that is why their eye is so clear-sighted, their judgment so incorruptible. They do not cry for the sake of crying or for the sake of the voice. Or because they begrudge earth's pleasant hours, exiled as they themselves are from the small warm companionships of the foreground. Theirs is the great comfort known only to those who have paced out the inmost and furthermost boundaries of existence.

They cry for blessing and salvation. They summon us to our last chance, while already they feel the ground quaking and the rafters creaking and see the firmest of mountains tottering inwardly and see the very stars in heaven hanging in peril. They summon us to the opportunity of warding off, by the greater power of a converted heart, the shifting desert that will pounce upon us and bury us.

O Lord, today we know once more, and in quite practical terms, what it means to clear away the rubble and make paths smooth again. We will have to know it and do it for years to come. Let the crying voices ring out, pointing out the wilderness and overcoming the devastation from within. May the Advent figure of John, the relentless envoy and prophet in God's name, be no stranger in our wilderness of ruins. For how shall we hear unless someone cries out above the tumult and destruction and delusion?

Advent comes in these three figures. This is not meant as an idyllic miniature painting, but as a challenge. My real concern is not with beautiful words, but with the truth. Let us kneel therefore and ask for the threefold blessing of Advent and its threefold inspiration.

Let us ask for clear eyes that are able to see God's messengers of annunciation; for awakened hearts with the wisdom to hear the words of promise. Let us ask for faith in the motherly consecration of life as shown in the figure of the blessed woman of Nazareth. Let us be patient and wait, wait with Advent readiness for the moment when it pleases God to appear in our night too, as the fruit and mystery of this time. And let us ask for the openness and willingness to hear God's warning messengers and to conquer life's wilderness through repentant hearts. We must not shrink from or suppress the earnest words of these crying voices, so that those who today are our executioners will not tomorrow become accusers because we have remained silent.

Let us then live in today's Advent, for it is the time of promise. To eyes that do not see, it still seems that the final dice are being cast down in these valleys, on these battlefields, in those camps and prisons and bomb shelters. Those who are awake sense the working of the other powers and can await the coming of their hour.

Space is still filled with the noise of destruction and annihilation, the shouts of self-assurance and arrogance, the weeping of despair and helplessness. But just beyond the horizon the eternal realities stand silent in their age-old longing. There shines on us the first mild light of the radiant fulfillment to come. From afar sound the first notes as of pipes and singing boys, not yet discernible as a song or melody. It is all far off still, and only just announced and foretold. But it is happening. This is today. And tomorrow the angels will tell what has happened with loud rejoicing voices, and we shall know it and be glad, if we have believed and trusted in Advent.

To Be Virgin

Loretta Ross-Gotta

LOTS OF PEOPLE these days are seeking recollection, writing books about it, urging us to do it. It seems like a nice idea all right – until you try it. What a lot of the books don't tell you about is the terror. To know the love of Christ that surpasses knowledge may mean not knowing much of anything else.

With the peace and quiet of recollection may come the stark edge of fear that this doing nothing, this being, this offering of oneself for God to be the actor, cannot possibly be enough. It all seems so passive. Do something, produce, perform, earn your keep. Don't just sit there. It may be good and well for Mary to offer space in herself for God to dwell and be born into the world, but few of us possess the radical belief such recollection requires.

What matters in the deeper experience of contemplation is not the doing and accomplishing. What matters is relationship, the being with. We create holy ground and give birth to Christ in our time not by doing but by believing and by loving the mysterious Infinite One who stirs within. This requires trust that something of great and saving importance is growing and kicking its heels in you.

The angel summoned Mary, betrothed to Joseph, from the rather safe place of conventional wisdom to a realm where few of the old rules would make much sense. She entered that unknown called "virgin territory." She was on her own there. No one else could judge for her the validity of her experience.

She can measure her reality against Scripture, the teachings of her tradition, her reason and intellect, and the counsel of wise friends. But finally it is up to her. The redemption of the creation is resting on the consent – the choice of this mortal woman to believe fearlessly that what she is experiencing is true. And to claim and live out that truth by conceiving the fruit of salvation.

To be virgin means to be one, whole in oneself, not perforated by the concerns of the conventional norms and authority, or the powers and principalities. To be virgin, then, is in a sense to be recollected.

Though recollection appears to be passive, it is worth noting that *conceive* is an active verb. Its Latin root means "to seize, to take hold of." Because Mary is recollected, she is able to take hold of God. Elizabeth, in whom John the Baptist leaps for joy at the approach of Christ in Mary, exclaims, "Blessed is she who believed that there would be fulfillment of what was spoken to her from the Lord." Blessed are all virgins, male and female, who believe that there will be fulfillment of what is spoken to them by the angelic messengers of grace.

Jesus observed, "Without me you can do nothing" (John 15:5). Yet we act, for the most part, as though without us God can do nothing. We think we have to make Christmas come, which is to say we think we have to bring about the redemption of the universe on our own. When all God needs is a willing womb, a place of safety, nourishment, and love. "Oh, but nothing will get done," you say. "If I don't do it,

Christmas won't happen." And we crowd out Christ with our fretful fears.

God asks us to give away everything of ourselves. The gift of greatest efficacy and power that we can offer God and creation is not our skills, gifts, abilities, and possessions. The wise men had their gold, frankincense, and myrrh, Paul and Peter had their preaching. Mary offered only space, love, belief. What is it that delivers Christ into the world – preaching, art, writing, scholarship, social justice? Those are all gifts well worth sharing. But preachers lose their charisma, scholarship grows pedantic, social justice alone cannot save us. In the end, when all other human gifts have met their inevitable limitation, it is the recollected one, the bold virgin with a heart in love with God who makes a sanctuary of her life, who delivers Christ who then delivers us.

Try it. Leave behind your briefcase and notes and proof texts. Leave behind your honed skills and knowledge. Leave the Christmas decorations up in the attic. Go to someone in need and say, "Here, all I have is Christ." And find out that that is enough.

Imagine a Christmas service where the worshipers come in their holiday finery to find a sanctuary empty of all the glittering decorations, silent of holiday carols. What if this year you canceled the church decoration committee and the worship committee and called off the extra choir rehearsals and the church school pageant?

What if on Christmas Eve people came and sat in the dim pews, and someone stood up and said, "Something happened here while we were all out at the malls, while we were baking cookies and fretting about whether we bought our brother-in-law the right gift: *Christ was born. God is here*"? We wouldn't need the glorious choruses and the harp and the bell choir and the organ. We wouldn't need the tree strung with lights. We wouldn't have to deny that painful dissonance between the promise and hope of Christmas and a world wracked with sin and evil. There wouldn't be that embarrassing conflict over the historical truth of the birth stories and whether or not Mary was really a virgin. And no one would have to preach sermons to work up our belief.

All of that would seem gaudy and shallow in comparison to the sanctity of that still sanctuary. And we, hushed and awed by something greater and wiser and kinder than we, would kneel of one accord in the stillness. A peace would settle over the planet like a velvet coverlet drawn over a sleeping child. The world would recollect itself and discover itself held in the womb of the Mother of God. We would be filled with all the fullness of God, even as we filled the emptiness of the Savior's heart with ours.

The intensity and strain that many of us bring to Christmas must suggest to some onlookers that, on the whole, Christians do not seem to have gotten the point of it. Probably few of us have the faith or the nerve to tamper with hallowed Christmas traditions on a large scale, or with our other holiday celebrations. But a small experiment might prove interesting. What if, instead of *doing* something, we were to *be* something special? Be a womb. Be a dwelling for God. Be surprised.

The Penitential Season

William Stringfellow

WE LIVE NOW, in the United States, in a culture so profoundly pagan that Advent is no longer really noticed, much less observed. The commercial acceleration of seasons, whereby the promotion of Christmas begins even before there is an opportunity to enjoy Halloween, is superficially, a reason for the vanishment of Advent. But a more significant cause is that the churches have become so utterly secularized that they no longer remember the topic of Advent. This situation cannot be blamed merely upon…the electronic preachers and talkers, or the other assorted peddlers of religion that so clutter the ethos of this society, any more than it can be said, simplistically, to be mainly the fault of American merchandising and consumerism.

Thus, if I remark about the disappearance of Advent I am not particularly complaining about the vulgarities of the marketplace prior to Christmas and I am certainly not talking about getting "back to God" or "putting Christ back into Christmas" (phrases that betray skepticism toward the Incarnation). Instead I am concerned with a single, straightforward question in biblical context, What is the subject of Advent?

Tradition has rendered John the Baptist an Advent figure and, if that be an appropriate connection (I reserve some queries about that), then clues to the meaning of the first coming of Christ may be found in the Baptist's preaching. Listen to John the Baptist.

"Repent, for the kingdom of heaven is at hand" (Matt. 3:2). In the Gospel according to Mark, the report is, John appeared in the wilderness, preaching a baptism of repentance for the forgiveness of sins. It should not be overlooked, furthermore, that when John the Baptist is imprisoned, Matthew states, "From that time Jesus began to preach, saying, 'Repent, for the kingdom of heaven is at hand' " (Matt. 4:17). And later, when Jesus charges his disciples, he tells them to preach the same message.

For all the greeting card and sermonic rhetoric, I do not think that much rejoicing happens around Christmastime, least of all about the coming of the Lord. There is, I notice, a lot of holiday frolicking, but that is not the same as rejoicing. In any case, maybe outbursts of either frolicking or rejoicing are premature, if John the Baptist has credibility. He identifies *repentance* as the message and the sentiment of Advent. And, in the texts just cited, that seems to be ratified by Jesus himself.

In context, in the biblical accounts, the repentance that John the Baptist preaches is no private or individualistic effort, but the disposition of a person is related to the reconciliation of the whole of creation. "Repent, for the kingdom of heaven is at hand."

The eschatological reference is quite concrete. John the Baptist is warning the rulers of this world and the principalities and powers, as well as common people, of the impending judgment of the world in the Word of God signaled in the coming of Christ…

The depletion of a contemporary recognition of the radically political character of Advent is in large measure occasioned by the illiteracy of church folk about the Second Advent and, in the mainline churches, the persistent quietism of pastors, preachers, and teachers about the Second Coming. That topic has been allowed to be preempted and usurped by astrologers, sectarian quacks, and multifarious hucksters. Yet it is impossible to apprehend either Advent except through the relationship of both Advents. The pioneer Christians, beleaguered as they were because of their insight, knew that the message of both Advents *is* political. That message is that in the coming of Jesus Christ, the nations and the principalities and the rulers of the world are judged in the Word of God. In the lordship of Christ they are rendered accountable to human life and, indeed, to all created life. Hence, the response of John the Baptist when he is pressed to show the meaning of the repentance he preaches is, "Bear fruits that befit repentance."

In another part of the Bible traditionally invoked during Advent, Luke 1: 52–54, the politics of both

Advents is emphasized in attributing the recitation of the Magnificat to Mary:

> He has put down the mighty from their thrones,
> and has exalted those of low degree;
> He has filled the hungry with good things,
> and the rich he has sent empty away.

In the First Advent, Christ the Lord comes into the world, in the next Advent, Christ the Lord comes as Judge of the world and of all the world's thrones and pretenders, sovereignties and dominions, principalities and authorities, presidencies and regimes, in vindication of his lordship and the reign of the Word of God in history. This is the truth, which the world hates, which biblical people (repentant people) bear and by which they live as the church in the world in the time between the two Advents.

From the Stable to the Cross

J. Heinrich Arnold, Edith Stein

JESUS' LIFE BEGAN in a stable and ended on the cross between two criminals. The Apostle Paul said he wanted to proclaim nothing but this crucified Christ. We, too, have nothing to hold on to except this Christ. We must ask ourselves again and again: Are we willing to go his way, from the stable to the cross? As disciples we are not promised comfortable and good times. Jesus says we must deny ourselves and suffer with him and for him. That is the only way to follow him, but behind it lies the glory of life – the glowing love of God, which is so much greater than our hearts and our lives.

J. HEINRICH ARNOLD

THE CHRISTIAN MYSTERIES are an indivisible whole. If we become immersed in one, we are led to all the others. Thus the way from Bethlehem leads inevitably to Golgotha, from the crib to the cross. When the blessed virgin brought the child to the temple, Simeon prophesied that her soul would be pierced by a sword, that this child was set for the fall and the resurrection of many, for a sign that would be contradicted. His prophecy announced the passion, the fight between light and darkness that already showed itself before the crib.

EDITH STEIN

Yielding to God

Philip Britts

WHEN THE WISE MEN, or the kings, came from the East, they went to Jerusalem, the capital, to inquire, "Where is he who has been born King of the Jews?" And today those who are "wise" make the same mistake in looking to worldly power to solve the world's problems. Others go to magnificent cathedrals and follow spiritual paths that appear much more splendid and much more clever than anything which accompanied the birth of Christ.

All this is misguided; it concentrates on the question of "how" instead of the question "why." We can easily get overwhelmed. How are we to carry out all the tasks laid upon us; how are we to plan our next year; how shall we find the strength both for securing our economic needs and in reaching out to the needs of others? But as important as these questions are, it is more important to remember the ancient question "Why?" Once we realize why Christ came to earth, why he was born as a helpless baby in a manger, and why his whole life was lived as an outcast from the best society, then can we begin to answer the question "how" – "how can we find God again; how can we experience peace on earth?"

We are human and finite, and thus cannot live perpetually in a sense of expectation, or in a continuous Advent. We are distracted by many things. Our spiritual awareness waxes and wanes in intensity. If an attitude of expectancy, or an inclination to poignant spiritual experiences, is cultivated by conscious effort of our own, we will suffer severe limitations. Such effort totally misses the mark. We may get lifted up in moments of tenderness but will be cast down in hours of dryness. The swing of emotions is natural to us, and some are more subject to extremes than others. We mustn't despair about this. But we should be aware of cultivating religious emotions under the delusion that these are the workings of the Holy Spirit. Such emotions are unstable; they risk getting in the way of our communion with God.

It is here that we need to see why it was necessary for Christ to come to the earth. God has come to us because we, by our own power of soul, by our own emotions, even the noblest and most sublime, can never attain redemption, can never regain communion with God.

True expectancy, the waiting that is genuine and from the heart, is brought about by the coming of the Holy Spirit, by God coming to us, and not by our own devices. Spiritual depth, if it is true, is the working of God coming down and penetrating to the depths of our hearts, and not of our own soul's climbing. No ladder of mysticism can ever meet or find or possess God. Faith is a power given to us. It is never simply our ability or strength of will to believe. The spiritual experience that is truly genuine is given to us by God in the coming of his Spirit, and only as we surrender our whole lives to an active expression of his will.

To put it quite simply, spiritual experience, whether it be of faith, hope (or expectancy) or love, is something we cannot manufacture, but which we can only receive. If we direct our lives to seeking it for ourselves we shall lose it, but if we lose our lives by living out the daily way of Christ we shall find it.

Spiritual experience, if it is of God, will indeed lead to a life of activity. But *the nature of the true activity is surrender and obedience.* The most striking revelation of this is found in the conception and birth of Jesus. When the angel Gabriel came to Mary, he told her, "The Holy Spirit shall come upon you, and the power of the Most High shall overshadow you." And she answered, "Behold the handmaiden of the Lord; be it unto me according to your word."

It was in this submission, this surrender and obedience, that Christ was conceived. And it is the laying down of power that is revealed in his birth. Christ did not spring armed from the head of Zeus. He came as a child. He was not even born in the protection of a royal court, with soldiers to guard against intruders and physicians to guard against sickness. Rather, he was born in a stable, at the mercy of Herod and the stark elements of cold and dirt.

This pattern of complete abandonment of human strength in total surrender to God's will is of vital importance for us, both in our lives of activity and of spiritual experience. It was in the surrender of herself to God that Mary became the mother of Christ. It was in her acceptance of Gabriel's message that the great decisive event of history took place. And in our own daily lives, in our efforts to do right, what is decisive is that we accept and live by and surrender ourselves to a strength which is not our own, to the piercing white light of God's love.

When we experience this love we turn away from the notion that we initiate and God responds; that we, by our religious efforts, can set something in motion that God must obey in response. To believe that by an effort of will we can mount nearer to God or add one cubit to our stature is as unchristian as the belief that we have no task as Christians for the mundane affairs of this world. Both beliefs have the same root – the pride that seeks to climb its way to God – and produces the same kind of confusion as the ancient attempt to build the tower of Babel.

The direction to which our wills must be put is in obedience to God's will in response to the breaking in of the Spirit. Then something decisive happens *for this earth*. In place of the confusion of injustice, strife, open war and treachery, there is revealed a path of the most lively unity and clarity. And in obediently following this path we are released from the servitude of our own desires, our selfish hopes and fears – we are redeemed, we become free.

If decisive and liberating Good is to be born on this earth, it must, like in Mary, find room in humble surrender. This does not mean a passive life of inaction. Far from it. The service of God makes the most impossible demands of us, demands which we know our strength cannot carry out, or which our hearts cannot bear. But our calling is obedience, even to the hardest demands; and we must take them up in the faith that our minds or bodies will be supported by the strength of God.

Although we are tempted to exert ourselves and push ourselves forward in our search for God, the desire to climb nearer to God is nothing but egotistical satisfaction and self-aggrandizement. The way that Christ took was the low way. His way is abandonment. He not only descended from the presence of God, but he came as a baby in the poorest conditions. It is not that we, as pilgrims, climb to a celestial city, but that the Christ child is born in the poverty of our hearts.

Surrender does not mean the cessation of seeking, for we must always seek the will of God in every situation. We seek in order to obey. And in obeying the small thing that we see, the greater is revealed to us. True surrender never separates itself from carrying out God's will.

This is why we do not come to know God by musing or by contemplating our highest ideals in splendid spiritual isolation, nor by disputing religious points and striving for a state of spiritual perfection. No, God comes to us when we offer a cup of water to the thirsty, whether it be plain water in an enamel cup or the water of life found in God's Word.

But let us not be deceived by such humble gestures. Human love cannot redeem. If it could there would have been no need for God to be born as a human child on this earth.

There is something altogether different from good will that we need. This something was fulfilled in the coming of Christ and in the manner of his coming. This amazing difference is fulfilled in our own lives when the Christ-child is born in our hearts. This is not an abstract experience or a flush of emotions, but a concrete acceptance of his Word. The birth of Christ is an example both unique and eternal of how the will of God is worked out on this earth. It is the birth of love in our hearts, which transforms life. God's love overwhelms us and breaks into our lives leaving our human good will behind. It was never Christ's purpose to bring about self-improvement. He became poor not to offer us a moral toning up, however good this may be. The Word became flesh so that the same amazing life that broke into the world when Jesus Christ was born actually becomes realized in our own lives here and now.

The meaning of Advent and Christmas is thus the coming down of God's love. This love alone revolutionizes our lives. Only God's love, not the elevation of human souls, can effect a transformation of the world. Those who mourn the futility of their own efforts receive the comfort of the love of God. Those who are meekly obedient to his will are filled by the love of God, not as a prize to be won after death, but as redeemed life for this earth.

Human love depends on human character and certain virtuous qualities. It propels some people to attain greater heights than others. A spiritual hierarchy is thus created in which each person climbs to a different height of godliness or saintliness according to his or her spiritual capacity. This is not the way of the manger. The love of God lays low all such hierarchy. Gifts, however spiritual, are not decisive. What is decisive is *agape*, the pure unconditional love of God.

Human love lifts up the Good Man. It is just this that Christ reveals as missing the point, when he himself, speaking as a man, says, "Why do you call me good? There is no one good but God." All our human goodness is relative; there is nothing in us immune from evil. Besides, Christ came not for the righteous but for sinners, for all those who can say, "Be it unto me according to your word."

The peace on earth the angels proclaimed is reconciliation with God. It is brought about by the coming of Christ into our poverty. In John's words, *"Herein is love: not that we loved God, but that he loved us."*

Mosaic of the Nativity

Serbia, Winter 1993

On the domed ceiling God
is thinking:
I made them my joy,
and everything else I created
I made to bless them.
But see what they do!
I know their hearts
and arguments:

"We're descended from
Cain. Evil is nothing new,
so what does it matter now
if we shell the infirmary,
and the well where the fearful

and rash alike must
come for water?"

God thinks Mary into being.
Suspended at the apogee
of the golden dome,
she curls in a brown pod,
and inside her the mind
of Christ, cloaked in blood,
lodges and begins to grow.

JANE KENYON

The Original Revolution

John Howard Yoder

IN THE WHOLE BODY of Jewish and Christian liturgy, only a very few texts might be more widely known – and more vainly repeated – than the two songs from the beginning of Luke's Gospel.

One of these songs is found on the lips of the maiden Mary. Catholic tradition knows it by its opening word *Magnificat*, "My soul doth magnify the Lord." But what it says is the language, not of sweet maidens, but of Maccabees: it speaks of dethroning the mighty and exalting the lowly, of filling the hungry and sending the rich away empty. Mary's praise to God is a revolutionary battle cry.

That simple observation should suffice to locate our topic. The fad word not long ago of both Protestant and Catholic social thought was "revolution." From the black ghettos of the U.S. to the 1968 World Council of Churches Assembly in Uppsala, from the archbishop's residence in Recife to the Ivy League seminaries of the American Protestant establishment, from Peking to the Sorbonne, the slogans are the same. The system is rotten. Those whom it oppresses should submit to its tyranny no longer. It deserves nothing other than to collapse in upon itself, a collapse we will engineer.

It would be worthwhile sometime to dwell at more length on the way in which the term "revolution" confirms the intellectual relevance of Gresham's law, according to which the coinage with the least substance, value, and character will get the most circulation. The word "revolution" has passed through so many hands, over so many tongues and pens, that most of its meaning has worn off. Shaving cream is revolutionary if they put lime perfume in the can with the soap… But the fact that a word can be prostituted or violated does not take its real meaning off our serious agenda.

The old word, the technical term, for the change Mary was rejoicing in is "gospel"; but "gospel" has become a tired old word. For some, it means the invitation to an individual to accept the forgiveness of sins, so that to preach the gospel, to "evangelize" is to spread the message of this invitation. For others, it means correct teaching about the work of Christ, so that "evangelicals" are those who hold to traditional doctrines. Elsewhere "evangelical" simply is the current word for "Protestant." For still others "gospel" represents a particular kind of country music.

If we are ever to rescue God's good news from all the justifiable but secondary meanings it has taken on, perhaps the best way to do it is to say that the root meaning of the term *evangelion* would today best be translated "revolution." Originally it is not a religious or a personal term at all, but a secular one: "good news." But *evangelion* is not just any welcome piece of information, it is news which impinges upon the fate of the community. "Good news" is the report brought by a runner to a Greek city, that a distant battle has been won, preserving their freedom; or that a son has been born to the king, assuring a generation of political stability. "Gospel" is good news having seriously to do with the people's welfare. Today we might speak of the end of the Vietnam war in this sense; not merely an event that makes some of us happy, but one which shapes our common lives for the better. This is not only true of the meaning of the word we translate "gospel," in its ordinary secular usage outside the New Testament; it is true as well of the story which the New Testament calls by this name. Mary's outburst of social enthusiasm in the *Magnificat* is only one sample; but the response of her kinsman Zechariah to the birth of his son is to sing that God has now come:

> ... age after age he proclaimed by the lips of his holy prophets, that he would deliver us from our enemies, out of the hands of all who hate us... (Luke 1:69–71)

When this son, John, began his own preaching, Luke describes it as "evangelizing the people" with predictions:

> Already the axe is laid to the roots of the trees, and every tree that fails to produce good fruit is cut down and thrown on the fire. (Luke 3:9)

To those who asked him, "What shall we do?" he answered:

> The man with two shirts must share with him who
> has none, and anyone who has food must do the
> same. (Luke 3:11)

Once again; whatever it is that God is about to do, it
will be good news for the poor, bad news for the
proud and the rich; it will be *change,* including
changed economic and social relations.

This was the expectation that Jesus himself
picked up, when in terms almost identical to John's,
he announced that the "kingdom of heaven is near"
and then more precisely:

> The spirit of the Lord is upon me, because he has
> anointed me; he has sent me to announce good
> news to the poor, to proclaim release for prisoners
> and recovery for the blind; to let the broken vic-
> tims go free, to proclaim the year of the Lord's
> favor. (Luke 4:18, 19)

The year of the Lord's favor of his "acceptable year"
is the Jubilee, the periodic economic leveling-off
provided for by the Mosaic law. Such a change is
what Jesus says is now coming into view in his beginning ministry. It will involve attitudes, so it can be

called "repentance," *metanoia*, "turning-the-mind-around." But it also involves social practices, "fruits worthy of repentance," new ways of using possessions and power. The promised coming change involves social and personal dimensions *inseparably*, with none of our modern speculative tendency to dodge the direct claim on us by debating whether the chicken or the egg comes first.

This was John's agenda, and Jesus'; but it is also ours. Between their time and ours, there have been other ages when men were more concerned with other questions, other priority agenda. There were centuries when men were especially aware of the fragility of life and its brevity; they wanted a word from God that would speak to their fear of death and the hereafter. Man's basic need was seen as his mortality. In this context it is no surprise that Christian preaching and poetry dealt with mortality and that the good news we needed was spoken in terms of eternal life.

In other societies and cultures, people are plagued by anxiety, guilt, fear of judgment. In this context the good news is stated in terms of forgiveness, acceptance by God, and acceptance by other men. Today some rephrase it as self-acceptance. In still other ages, other cultures, man thinks of his need as primarily for help in getting a job or in facing sickness or poverty. To this as well the Christian message can speak. People are still asking these questions, and Christian preachers are still proclaiming good news in all these ways; why should they not?

But for Jesus in his time, and for increasing numbers of us in our time, the basic human problem is seen in less individualistic terms. The priority agenda for Jesus, and for many of us, is not mortality or anxiety, but unrighteousness, injustice. The need is not for consolation or acceptance but for a new order in which men may live together in love. In his time, therefore, as in ours, the question of revolution, *the judgment of God upon the present order and the imminent promise of another one*, is the language in which the gospel must speak. What most people *mean* by "revolution," the *answer* they want, is not the gospel; but the gospel, if it be authentic, must so speak as to answer the *question* of revolution. This Jesus did.

Christmas Joy

Emmy Arnold

TO BECOME LIKE CHILDREN! The most beautiful childhood memory that comes to my mind is that of celebrating Christmas and the joy of Christmas.

Perhaps my experiences of Christmas came from the fact that I was born on Christmas Day. A hundred days before each Christmas we children would begin to count the days. Only a hundred times more I will wake up in the morning, and then, hurrah! it's Christmas Day! When at six o'clock on the eve of the First Sunday of Advent the bells rang in the Advent season, it seemed as though the angels were exulting, and we little earthly children joined in. "O welcome, thou blessed Christmas time!"

From then on, the joy and eagerness for what was to come mounted with each day. Sometimes in the evening, when I was looking out into the darkness of the still night, I would think I saw God's angels coming down to proclaim the Christmas message to us. The breath of Christmas peace blew down like a greeting from heaven; all the sounds that were part of this time turned into Christmas music.

Lift up your heads, ye mighty gates;
Behold, the Lord of glory comes!

Even though the celebration of Christmas is exploited for business profit and used for selfish purposes; even though the meaning of Christmas is often corrupted; in spite of all this, we all feel the impulse at this time to think of others, to show love to others, to be there for others. This itself shows what this joy of anticipation is. It is the feeling of human solidarity, the exulting joy in one another, the certainty of mutual love. The brightness and fragrance of the living Christmas tree under which Christmas gifts are laid – here is light and warmth, symbolizing life and love.

A child, thinking of these Christmas symbols and Christmas gifts, might ask himself, Is all this something that can go away? Can this be just an excitement that soon fades away? No, is the answer within him; for all this is not yet the best, and the best cannot pass. "To us a Child is born, to us a Son is given." "God so loved the world that He gave His only Son." Of all gifts there is none so precious as this one. Therefore we ask only for this one gift: Stay with us, Lord Jesus Christ!

When as a child I stood before the lighted crib scene, I often fell into a deep reverie. I saw the Christ Child in his eternal light; I felt the same that the shepherds felt when they came to the crib to worship the little Child. It was there that I first realized what the joy of worship means. God's greatness came in the smallness of the Child in the crib.

When in awe my heart is still
and tries to grasp this miracle,
all I can do is pray to God
and feel how endless is His love.

God became man for our own sake;
God's Child, with us in flesh united.

Arnold · 129

How could God hate us, when He gives
us what He, past all measure, loves?

Love Him who with love is burning,
See the Star who on us pours
Light and comfort!

Anyone who as a child has looked into God's loving
heart can never despair of his life, however hard it
may be.

Joy radiates peace. Love brings peace. "I proclaim
to you great joy that shall come to all peoples –
peace on earth!" The true Christmas experience is to
feel that this Christmas peace is the greater power;
that even now on earth it overcomes all unpeace.
That this peace shall come to all – that is the expectation and the faith of Christmas!

The Christmas Star in the night sky, the shining
of the Christmas light in the night – all this is the
sign that light breaks into the darkness. Though we
see about us the darkness of unrest, of family discord,
of class struggle, of competitive jealousy and of na-
tional hatred, the light shall shine and drive it out.
"The people who walked in darkness have seen a

great light; those who dwelt in a land of deep darkness, on them has light shined."

Jesus is the light. Nobody else is the light; others
can only witness to the light.

The eternal light shall come to earth
and give it a new radiance;
it shines into the midst of night
and makes us children of the light.

Only those who are reborn as children shall become
children of the light. Wherever the Christmas Child
is born in a heart, wherever Jesus begins his earthly
life anew – that is where the life of God's love and of
God's peace dawns again.

To Believe

Karl Barth

Then the angel of the Lord appeared to Zechariah, standing at the right side of the altar of incense. When Zechariah saw him, he was startled and was gripped with fear. But the angel said to him: "Do not be afraid, Zechariah; your prayer has been heard. Your wife Elizabeth will bear you a son, and you are to give him the name John..."

Zechariah asked the angel, "How can I be sure of this? I am an old man and my wife is well along in years."

The angel answered, "I am Gabriel. I stand in the presence of God, and I have been sent to speak to you and to tell you this good news. And now you will be silent and not able to speak until the day this happens, because you did not believe my words, which will come true at their proper time."

Meanwhile, the people were waiting for Zechariah and wondering why he stayed so long in the temple. When he came out, he could not speak to them. They realized he had seen a vision in the temple, for he kept making signs to them but remained unable to speak.

LUKE 1:11–22

THERE ARE SO MANY GATES and doors that must finally be lifted high and opened wide, and there are still many prisoners who must finally be set free. For truly we are among the prisoners, and among the gates that should be opened, I include our closed ears and lips. Our lips! Because we are actually quite similar to poor Zechariah, of whom we have just read. After all, something burns in our hearts that would gladly come out. Something often flames up in our soul that we would like to call out to all people – a question, a complaint, a word of defiance, a rejoicing, a stark truth – something of the sort that a person simply cannot keep to himself, once it is there.

It saddens us to be so alone, to be unable to share with anyone what moves us. It also saddens us to see other people coming and going, all in their own way, all in so much error and dullness when we have something to tell them that would help them. For we sense that their concern is at root our own concern.

Above all it saddens us that we are so cut off from each other, that there are always such different worlds – you in your house and me in my house, you with your thoughts and me with mine. This is simply not the way life is meant to be, this separate life we all lead. But with one single change we could have infinitely more joy and good fortune and righteousness among us, if we could open our hearts and talk with each other.

And then we experience the fact that we are mute. Yes, we certainly talk with each other, we find words all right, but never the right words; never the words that would really do justice to what actually moves us, what actually lives in us; never the words that would really lead us out of our loneliness into community. Our talk is always such an imperfect, wooden, dead talk. Fire will not break out in it, but can only smolder in our words.

Hearing the story of Zechariah, I immediately have to think of myself. I have so often climbed up into the pulpit, and experienced just what is said here: "And when Zechariah came out, he could not speak with them, and they realized that he had seen a vision in the Temple. And he made signs to them and remained dumb." I once thought it so easy to preach, but now it strikes me as harder and harder to say what needs to be said. All the better do I understand the men of the Bible, Moses and Jeremiah and others who beseeched God not to make them speak of him, because they simply could not. All our lips are bound. And my plight is also your plight. I am not able to speak, because you too are not able. You do not speak with me either. What you say to me is at most only an incomprehensible gesture; I hear only words. O, our closed up lips! Who can finally open them for us!

Zechariah was mute because he did not believe the angel. We all are just like Zechariah in the sanctuary. Every one of us has a hidden side of our being that is, as it were, in touch with God. We are secretly in a close connection with the eternal truth and love, even if we ourselves are not aware of it. And from this other hidden side of our being resounds a voice that is actually speaking to us constantly. "Gabriel, who stands before God," spoke to Zechariah. We could think of the words of Jesus, that even the least have an angel who always beholds the face of the Father in heaven (Mt. 18:10). This angel stands before God, but sometimes, in the sanctuary, he also stands right before us. He speaks with God, but he also speaks with us.

However else we think about it, the living word of God is available to us. It is a word that, in contrast to all human words, is clear, intelligible and unambiguous. Yes, this inward word of God, which God speaks to us by means of his angels, contains precisely that which so moves and unsettles us. It is this word that so delights and grieves us, and which we would so gladly tell one another.

Without this word we would not suffer so deeply from the need that presses in upon us, and from the injustice that we must stand by and watch. We would not be able to resist so powerfully and become so indignant against the lies and violence that we see dominating life apart from this word. We would not have the urge to exercise love and to become loving if it were not for the fact that within us is God's voice, placed into our heart. In this way God spoke to Zechariah of something quite grand – a coming great decision and turning of all things, of the approaching better age at hand, of the Savior meant to become a helper for the people, and of his herald, whose father he himself would become.

Even if we have never seen angels standing "on the right of the incense altar," the fire of God can actually burn us, the earthquake of God can still shake us, the flood of God awaits to rush around us, the storm of God actually wants to seize us. O, if we could actually hear, if we could but hear this voice that resounds so clearly within us as actually God's voice. If we could only believe. Then we could also speak. As Psalm 116:10 says: I believe, therefore I also speak.

Believing is not something as special and difficult or even unnatural as we often suppose. Believing means that what we listen to, we listen to as God's speech. What moves us is not just our own concern, but precisely God's concern. What causes me worry, that is God's worry, what gives me joy is God's joy, what I hope for is God's hope. In other words, in all that I am, I am only a party to that which God thinks and does. In all that I do it is not I, but rather God who is important. Imagine if everything were brought into this great and proper connection, if we were willing to suffer, be angry, love and rejoice with God, instead of always wanting to make everything our own private affair, as if we were alone.

Just imagine if we were to adapt everything that gratifies and moves us into the life and movement of God's kingdom, so that we personally are, so to speak, taken out of play. Simply love! Simply hope! Simply rejoice! Simply strive! But in everything, do it no longer from yourself, but rather from God! Everything great that is hidden in you can indeed be great only in God.

Don't you think we would learn to talk with one another if we would cease speaking about our own separate concerns; if the human would cease putting itself in front of the divine? What would happen to us if we approached each other thinking: what he is saying is not on his own, but rather on a higher authority, not because he wants to, but because he must. Wouldn't we then once and for all find the words, the right words? Might we not be able to truly hear and understand?

God's thoughts are in us and over us. Yet we must learn to believe, believe that everything depends upon the God who stands behind us; we are in his hand. The greatest, the best in us is precisely not our own private concern, but rather God's. Ah, if I could only believe it! It need not be complicated. Let the divine that you do recognize actually be divine for once! Or perhaps you and I like our insecurity and instability compared to the thoughts of God. Perhaps we prefer to place ourselves next to the truth instead of in the truth?

We must once and for all give up trying to be self-made individuals. Let us cease preaching by ourselves, being right by ourselves, doing good by ourselves, being sensible by ourselves, improving the world by ourselves. God wants to do everything, certainly through us and with us and never without us; but our participation in what he does must naturally originate and grow out of his power, not ours. O, how we could then speak with one another. For whatever does not grow out of God produces smoke, not fire. But that which is born of God overcomes the world (1 Jn. 5:4). We only need to speak with our fellow men on the basis of faith. So long as our words do not arise from faith, from our confidence in the power of

God, we will be and remain mute. Only faith can speak. But faith *can* speak! This is how our ears must be opened and then also our mouths.

So now here we stand, simultaneously deaf and mute like Zechariah. Ah yes, we only want to pretend to be next to him. In spite of his unbelief, he was still a herald of Advent, one who waited for God. Otherwise the angel would not have spoken with him. Nor would he have become the father of John the Baptist. When everything came to pass which he could not believe and could not express, then he was suddenly able to believe and speak. For God does not stand still when we come to a standstill, but precedes us with his deeds and only waits so that we can follow. And so we will accept – even with all that we cannot say, and with all that we have not yet heard – that we are also heralds of Advent. We will finally believe, and then we will also hear.

The God We Hardly Knew

William Willimon

No one can celebrate
a genuine Christmas
without being truly poor.
The self-sufficient, the proud,
those who, because they have
everything, look down on others,
those who have no need
even of God – for them there
will be no Christmas.
Only the poor, the hungry,
those who need someone
to come on their behalf,

will have that someone.
That someone is God.
Emmanuel. God-with-us.
Without poverty of spirit
there can be no abundance of God.

OSCAR ROMERO

PROBABLY MOST OF US have had the experience of receiving, right out of the blue, a gift from someone we really don't know all that well. And perhaps, to our consternation, the gift turns out to be nice, something that we didn't know we wanted and certainly didn't ask for, but there it is, a good gift from someone who is not really a good friend. Now, what is the first thing we do in response?

Right. We try to come up with a gift to give in return – not out of gratitude (after all we didn't ask for it) or out of friendship (after all we hardly knew this person), but because we don't want to feel guilty.

We don't want to be indebted. The gift seems to lay a claim upon us, especially since it has come from someone we barely know. This is uncomfortable; it's hard to look the person in the face until we have reciprocated. By giving us a gift, this person has power over us.

It may well be, as Jesus says, more blessed to give than to receive. But it is more difficult to receive. Watch how people blush when given a compliment. Watch what you do when your teen-aged son comes home with a very expensive Christmas present from a girl he has dated only twice. "Now you take that expensive sweater right back and tell her that your parents won't allow you to accept it. Every gift comes with a claim and you're not ready for her claim upon you." In a society that makes strangers of us all, it is interesting what we do when a stranger gives us a gift.

And consider what we do at Christmas, the so-called season of giving. We enjoy thinking of ourselves as basically generous, benevolent, giving people. That's one reason why everyone, even the nominally religious, loves Christmas. Christmas is a season to celebrate our alleged generosity. The newspaper keeps us posted on how many needy families we have adopted. The Salvation Army kettles enable us to be generous while buying groceries (for ourselves) or gifts (for our families). People we work with who usually balk at the collection to pay for the morning coffee fall over themselves soliciting funds "to make Christmas" for some family.

We love Christmas because, as we say, Christmas brings out the best in us. Everyone gives on Christmas, even the stingiest among us, even the Ebenezer Scrooges. Charles Dickens' story of Scrooge's transformation has probably done more to form our notions of Christmas than St. Luke's story of the manger. Whereas Luke tells us of God's gift to us, Dickens tells us how we can give to others. A *Christmas Carol* is more congenial to our favorite images of ourselves. Dickens suggests that down deep, even the worst of us can become generous, giving people.

Yet I suggest we are better givers than getters, not because we are generous people but because we are proud, arrogant people. The Christmas story – the one according to Luke not Dickens – is not about how blessed it is to be givers but about how essential it is to see ourselves as receivers.

We prefer to think of ourselves as givers – powerful, competent, self-sufficient, capable people whose goodness motivates us to employ some of our power, competence and gifts to benefit the less fortunate. Which is a direct contradiction of the biblical account of the first Christmas. There we are portrayed not as the givers we wish we were but as the receivers we are. Luke and Matthew go to great lengths to demonstrate that we – with our power, generosity, competence and capabilities – had little to do with God's work in Jesus. God wanted to do something for us so strange, so utterly beyond the bounds of human imagination, so foreign to human projection, that God had to resort to angels, pregnant virgins, and stars in the sky to get it done. We didn't think of it, understand it or approve it. All we could do, at Bethlehem, was receive it. A gift from a God we hardly even knew.

This theme struck me forcefully a few years ago while counseling someone from my church. It was December. She was telling me about her worry and confusion over a number of problems. Having taken several counseling courses in seminary, I knew how to be a good counselor. That is, I knew to keep quiet, listen patiently, ask questions, and offer no direct guidance. After I had given her ample opportunity to vent her feelings, I remarked as I had been taught: "I believe that you have the solution to your problems within you. I believe that down deep, you know what your real problem is and that you have the re-sources to handle it."

You have heard the message before. One certainly does not have to come to church to hear this popu-lar gospel: You have, within you, the solution to what ails you.

And then it hit me. It was the middle of Decem-ber, late in Advent. In less than two weeks I would be standing in front of the congregation reading the nativity story from one of the Gospels, demonstrat-ing through a strange story of a virgin birth to a peas-ant couple in Judea that the solution to what ails us has very little to do with us. After having tried for generations to cure what ails us, God reached for something inconceivable. God put on our back door-step a solution so radical that many missed it.

Rabbi Michael Goldberg, in his book *Jews and Christians*, says that as a Jew he is impressed in read-ing Matthew's account of the nativity by how utterly passive the actors are. As a Jew, he answers to the story of the Exodus, a story of how God liberated the chosen people through the enlistment and prodding of people like Moses, Aaron and Miriam. But the Christmas story implies that what God wants to do for us is so strange, so beyond the bounds of human effort and striving, that God must resort to utterly unnatural, supernatural means. It tells of an unimaginable gift from a stranger, a God whom we hardly even knew.

This strange story tells us how to be receivers. The first word of the church, a people born out of so odd a nativity, is that we are receivers before we are givers. Discipleship teaches us the art of seeing our lives as gifts. That's tough, because I would rather see myself as a giver. I want power – to stand on my own, take charge, set things to rights, perhaps to help those who have nothing. I don't like picturing myself as dependent, needy, empty-handed.

Working with students at a university, I've decided that this truth is a major reason why many children come to despise their parents. It's humbling to see one's life, talents, capabilities, values, weaknesses and strengths as gifts from one's parents. We would rather be self-made men and women, standing on our own feet, striding bravely into a new world of our creation. It's humbling to look into a mirror at twenty-one and admit, "My God, I look just like my old man."

I suspect that the difficulty of receiving is a factor in marriage, too. It's painful to be thrust into such close proximity to another human being, day after day, year after year, until one gradually comes to see that one's identity and character are due to an alarming degree, to what one has received from one's spouse. Marriage is an everyday experience of living in the red – debtors to someone whom we have just begun to know.

If one asks the Gift Records Office of my school who are our most antagonistic alumni, they'll tell you they are the ones who were here on full scholarship. We talk a great deal about "right to life," "freedom of choice" and "self-determination," but not too much about indebtedness.

It's tough to be on the receiving end of love, God's or anybody else's. It requires that we see our lives not as our possessions, but as gifts. "Nothing is more repugnant to capable, reasonable people than grace," wrote John Wesley a long time ago.

Among the most familiar Christmas texts is the one in Isaiah: "The Lord himself will give you a sign. Behold, a young woman shall conceive and bear a son, and shall call his name Emmanuel" (Isaiah

7:14). Less familiar is its context: Isaiah has been pleading with King Ahaz to put his trust in God's promise to Israel rather than in alliances with strong military powers like Syria. "If you will not believe, you shall not be established," Isaiah warns Ahaz (7:9). Then the prophet tells the fearful king that God is going to give him a baby as a sign. A baby. Isn't that just like God, Ahaz must have thought. What Ahaz needed, with Assyria breathing down his neck, was a good army, not a baby.

This is often the way God loves us: with gifts we thought we didn't need, which transform us into people we don't necessarily want to be. With our advanced degrees, armies, government programs, material comforts and self-fulfillment techniques, we assume that religion is about giving a little of our power in order to confirm to ourselves that we are indeed as self-sufficient as we claim.

Then this stranger comes to us, blesses us with a gift, and calls us to see ourselves as we are — empty-handed recipients of a gracious God who, rather than leave us to our own devices, gave us a baby.

Be Not Afraid

Johann Christoph Arnold

PERFECT LOVE, the apostle John writes, casts out fear. So when God's angel broke the good news of the Savior's birth to the cowering shepherds of Bethlehem, "Fear not!" was more than an instruction for them to get up off the ground and stop shielding their frightened faces. It was a declaration of war on fear. The "glad tidings of great joy, which shall be to all people" meant that fear's grip on human hearts was going to have to give way to the far greater power of love.

People have derived comfort from these words for two thousand years, but millions of us are still afraid. What's more, we are scared to admit our fears, particularly our biggest fear of all – death.

The fear of death overshadows all our lives. We live longer than our grandparents; we are better fed; we lose fewer babies. Vaccines protect us from once-feared epidemics; hi-tech hospitals save tiny pre-emies and patients in need of a new kidney or heart. But we are still mortal. And even if we have been successful in warding off plagues that decimated earlier generations, we have no lack of our own, from addiction, suicide, abortion, and divorce to racism, poverty, violence, and militarism. We live, as Pope John Paul II has said, in a culture of death.

It is also a culture of fear. Fearing old age, we hide our elderly in nursing homes. Fearing crime, we protect ourselves with guns and locked doors. Fearing people who don't look like us or earn as much, we move into segregated or "gated" neighborhoods. Fearing other nations, we impose sanctions and drop bombs. We are even afraid of our own offspring, turning our schools into virtual prisons, and our prisons into holding pens and morgues. Add to all these anxieties several more that are driving millions to distraction: terrorism, bio-warfare, and planes falling out of the sky.

I live in New York, and after September 11, 2001,

the words "fear not" seemed out of place, even cruel. Surely we had every reason to be afraid. But somehow I couldn't get those words out of my head, especially when I thought of my friend Father Mychal Judge, a Franciscan priest and fire department chaplain – and the first registered victim at Ground Zero, the site of the former Twin Towers. The details of his death are unclear: some say he was fatally wounded as he administered last rites to a dying firefighter; others remember him standing alone in silent prayer. Whatever happened, his lifeless body was discovered in the lobby and carried to a nearby church shortly before Tower One collapsed.

Father Mike had poured his heart into his chaplaincy work for the Fire Department of New York and was an outspoken advocate for people dying of AIDS; he was also known throughout the city for his love of the downtrodden. With a pocketful of dollar bills "rescued" from friends who could afford to give them away, he always had something to give a needy person on the street. In 1999, Father Mike and I traveled through Northern Ireland with a mutual friend, NYPD Detective Steven McDonald, promoting dialogue and reconciliation. We made a second trip to Ireland in 2000, and at the time of his death, we were in the final stages of planning a similar one to Israel and the West Bank.

When I thought of Father Mike, it occurred to me that here was a man who had arrived at Ground Zero long before that fateful September morning. He had loved life with his whole being, but he had also proved himself ready many times before to "lay down his life for his friends" – like the time he climbed a ladder to the window of a second-floor apartment, and talked a frenzied gunman into surrendering to police. It was easy for me to imagine Father Mike spending his last moments on earth encouraging another person by turning him toward God, away from fear. He had been doing that all his life. When I think of Father Mike, I feel certain that God was there in lower Manhattan on 9/11, with every soul, in the midst of that sheer terror and raw evil. This gives me comfort.

If the thought of finding God in such horrendous circumstances seems strange, perhaps it is because we are out of practice looking for him. In good times it is easy for us to call God "Father" and acknowledge him as the source of our blessings. But when tragedy strikes we too often (to borrow from George Mac-Donald) "look upon God as our last and feeblest resort. We go to him because we have nowhere else to go." We forget that God is right there, waiting for us to turn to him, no matter how dire our situation. And we forget the reassuring words of his messengers: "Fear not." If we really trusted in God, these words would never seem empty. Instead, they would remind us that God always seeks to draw close to us – even, as the Psalmist writes, in the depths of hell. And they might also remind us that (to quote MacDonald again) once we do turn to God we will find that the storms of life have "driven us not upon the rocks but unto our desired haven."

Many people may feel God wasn't there on September 11. They see the world as an increasingly frightening place. Their faith has been shaken. I know how they feel. I have eight children and some two dozen grandchildren, and I know what it is like to ponder the future and be scared. I have also stood at the bedside of dying friends and relatives – and have fought alongside them – as they faced death. I have held their hands when fear filled their eyes, and have witnessed the remarkable peace that radiates from those who have not only battled their fears, but found strength to ask God to intervene on their behalf.

Without exception, these were ordinary men and women who at some point in their life had decided to spend their energies reaching out to people around them, rather than focusing on themselves. Through this, they received a special gift: the ability to hear the angel's words, "Fear not!" Such a gift can only be given to a surrendered heart, one that knows itself to be held in the palm of God's hand.

My grandfather, writer Eberhard Arnold, was one such person. He grasped intuitively that our flesh, blood, and bones are not, in the truest and deepest sense, our real selves, but that the real seat of our being, the soul, passes from mortality into immortality, and from time into timelessness. My grandfather spoke of the human soul's perpetual longing for God, and referred to death as the moment we are "called into eternity" and united with God.

It is natural, even for us who call ourselves believers, to feel the gulf between our present state and eternal unity with God. But then we should bear in mind that the angel's "glad tidings," wonderful as they are, do not spell out the whole story. Christ's life began in a manger, but its pivotal point was his crucifixion, and its completion was Easter, when he rose from the dead.

Many years of counseling people through grief and loss have made me certain that Christ's death and resurrection hold the deepest answer to all our fears. We all have bad days; and plenty of us know what depression is. There are very few people who have not, at one time or another, experienced deep anguish – and growing numbers have faced the terror of violence. In our lives we may be tested in ways we cannot even imagine. Yet we can be certain Christ has shared our torment, and worse. He sweated drops of blood and was totally forsaken. He died, and descended into hell. But by overcoming death he took away all our reasons for fear, forever.

Of course, it does no good to recognize this in a merely intellectual way. Knowing that Christ loves us may not save us from fear, nor will it save us from death. And so it comes down to this: the only way to truly overcome our fear of death is to live life in such a way that its meaning cannot be taken away by death.

This sounds grandiose, but it is really very simple. It means fighting the impulse to live for ourselves, instead of for others. It means choosing generosity over greed. It also means living humbly, rather than seeking influence and power. Finally, it means being ready to die again and again – to ourselves, and to every self-serving opinion or agenda.

In Dickens's *Christmas Carol*, the bitter old accountant Scrooge provides a memorable illustration. Tight-fisted and grasping, he goes through life dragging a chain that he himself has forged, link by link, with each miserly deed. Having closed himself to human kindness, he lives in a universe so calculating and cold that no one escapes his suspicion. Before long he begins to despise himself and look for a way out of his misery. But he cannot find one. He is trapped – trapped in the prison of self. Worse, he is haunted by dreams of death, and dreads its approach.

Then he changes. Loosened by those same dreams, the scales fall from his eyes, and he sees a way out: "The time before him was his own, to make amends in!" No longer consumed with his own needs, he is free to love, and vows to dispel "the shadows of the things that would have been." And as he runs from one old acquaintance to the next, he rediscovers the world around him with the unself-conscious happiness of a child.

Such happiness can be ours, too, if we live for love. By "love" I am not speaking simply of the emotion, nor of some grand, abstract ideal, but of the life-changing power Jesus speaks of when he says: "I was hungry and you gave me food, I was thirsty and you gave me drink, I was a stranger and you welcomed me, I was naked and you clothed me, I was sick and you visited me, I was in prison and you came to me" (Mt. 25: 35–36).

Love is a tangible reality. Sometimes it is born of passion or devotion; sometimes it demands hard work and sacrifice. Its source is unimportant. But when we live for love, we will be able to meet any challenge that comes our way – even the final one, of death.

As my great-aunt Else lay dying of tuberculosis, a friend asked her if she had one last wish. She replied, "Only to love more." If we live our lives in love, we will know peace now, and at the hour of death. And we will not be afraid.

Genealogy and Grace

Gail Godwin

It's a Sunday morning shortly before Christmas at All Saints Episcopal, a small-town church in the Smoky Mountains. The narrator, Margaret, is the local priest; Jennifer, the teenage daughter of a close friend, has been asked to read the genealogy of Jesus at the ten-o'clock service:

JENNIFER MOUNTED to the pulpit. I had instructed her to count to twenty silently before she began to read, and I could feel her honoring every digit, despite her eagerness to start.

"The Genealogy of Jesus Christ, from the first chapter of Matthew. The story of the origin of Jesus Christ, son of David, son of Abraham:

Abraham was the father of Isaac;
Isaac was the father of Jacob;
Jacob was the father of Judah and his brothers;
Judah was the father of Perez and Zerah by Tamar;
Perez was the father of Hezron;
Hezron was the father of Aram;
Aram was the father of Amminadab;
Amminadab was the father of Nahshon;
Nahshon was the father of Salmon;
Salmon was the father of Boaz by Rahab;
Boaz was the father of Obed by Ruth;
Obed was the father of Jesse;
Jesse was the father of David the king;
David was the father of Solomon by Uriah's wife;
Solomon was the father of Rehoboam;
Rehoboam was the father of Abijah…"

The baffled looks could be seen kicking in before Jennifer got to Amminadab and had spread over most faces by the time she reached Rehoboam. If I had dared to do this part of the sermon, there would have been raised eyebrows before Perez and silent mutiny before Boaz. The novelty was this handsome girl in her alb, graciously doling out the unpronounceable and obscure names in her precise, ring-ing voice as if they had been one-of-a-kind charms handmade by herself for them to take home and hang on their Christmas trees. Added to the attrac-tion was that everyone knew her; many had been present yesterday at the triumphal acquisition of a new mother.

The recitation of the genealogy took three min-utes and ten seconds. Jennifer had clocked it before-hand with her stopwatch. By the time she had launched, with Jeconiah, into the final fourteen-generation home stretch to Jesus, most faces were alternating between polite resignation and piqued interest ("What is Pastor Margaret going to spring on us now?"). The exceptions were Chase Zorn, whose eyes were riveted on Jennifer, and his pew neighbor Grace Munger, whose haughty counte-nance maintained an emphatic attention through-out; periodically she gave small brisk nods, as though she wanted it clear that all of these names were per-fectly familiar to her.

"Thus the total generations from Abraham to David were fourteen generations, and from David to the Babylonian Exile fourteen more generations, and finally from the Babylonian Exile to Christ fourteen more generations."

Jennifer bowed and returned to her server's bench and I replaced her in the pulpit.

"Back when I was in seminary in New York, I once heard Raymond Brown, the Roman Catholic priest and scholar, give a talk on preparing for Advent. I was so struck with his insights that I forgot to take notes and could have kicked myself later. But last summer when I was away in New York, I came across a monograph of his, *A Coming of Christ in Advent*, in my seminary's bookstore, and guess what? Inside was the 'lost lecture' in the form of an essay. There's no way I can do justice to all of it, but I do want to touch on the points that were so illuminating to me. If anyone's appetite is whetted for more, the monograph will be on the library shelves in the crypt.

"As you know, we have two stories of Jesus' conception and birth. Only two, Matthew's and Luke's, and they are very different from each other. When we reread them, it comes as a shock to some of us just *how* different. Did Mary and Joseph live in a house in Bethlehem where Jesus was born; or did they live in Nazareth and go to register for a Roman census in

Bethlehem, where Jesus was born in a stable because the inn was full? Did they flee from their house in Bethlehem into Egypt to escape Herod's child-killing rampage after he had been tipped off by the magi's arrival; or did they return peacefully home to Nazareth after the Bethlehem census-taking with nary a mention of Herod?

"Our Christmas pageants usually combine the two stories, but when biblical scholars attempt to reconcile the conflicting material they can't. Raymond Brown suggests that we might do better to recognize that the Holy Spirit was content to give us two different accounts and that the way to interpret them faithfully is to treat them separately. Not try to force a harmony out of some mistaken notion that if scripture is inspired it has to be historical as well...

"In his monograph Father Brown writes that he's been conducting a somewhat solitary campaign to urge pastors to preach the Matthean genealogy during Advent. And I'm finally getting around to doing it, now that I'm a pastor myself. He says that these three minutes worth of tongue twisting names contain the essential theology of the Old and New

Testaments for the whole Church, Orthodox, Roman Catholic, and Protestant alike.

"Now that's a pretty bold and sweeping ecumenical statement. But Brown tells us Zwingli was already preaching it back during the Reformation. Zwingli preached that Matthew's genealogy contained the essential theology of the Reformation: that of salvation by grace.

"The 'story of the origin of Jesus Christ' begins with Abraham begetting Isaac; no mention of that deserving elder son, poor unfairly banished Ishmael. Then Isaac begets Jacob; not a word about his elder brother Esau whose birthright Jacob stole. Jacob begets Judah and his brothers; why is Judah chosen and not the good and extraordinary Joseph?

"What's going on here? According to Matthew, who is being faithful to Old Testament theology, God does not necessarily select the noblest or most deserving person to carry out divine purposes.

"Now that's the interesting part. For reasons unknown to us, God may select the Judahs who sell their brothers into slavery, the Jacobs who cheat their way to first place, the Davids who steal wives and murder rivals – but also compose profound and beautiful psalms of praise.

"And what about the five women Matthew chooses to include? Not a mention of Sarah or Rebekah or Rachel, the upstanding patriarchal wives of Israel. Instead *Tamar*, a Cananite, who disguised herself as a prostitute and seduced her father-in-law Judah to get a son out of him. And *Rahab*, another Cananite and a real prostitute this time. And *Ruth* the Moabite, another outsider. And *Bathsheba*, mother of Solomon, is named only as the wife of Uriah, whom King David had killed so he could marry her himself. Every one of these women used as God's instrument had scandal or aspersion attached to her – as does the fifth and final woman named in the genealogy: *Mary*, the mother of Jesus, with her unconventional pregnancy.

"But this will fit in with Jesus' coming ministry to tax collectors and sinners and prostitutes and lepers, 'to those who need a physician,' not those who are already righteous.

"Matthew's genealogy is showing us how the story of Jesus Christ contained – and would continue to contain – the flawed and inflicted and insulted, the cunning and the weak-willed and the misunderstood.

"His is an equal opportunity ministry for crooks and saints.

"And what about that final fourteen generations of unknown, or unremarkable, names Jennifer read to us? Who was Azor, or Achim? Who was Eliud, who was Eliezar? Or even this Mathan, who was according to Matthew, Jesus' great grandfather? What did they do? What kind of men were they? We don't know. You won't find their names in the concordance, or in any biblical *Who's Who.*

"And this is of course, where the message settles directly upon us. If so much powerful stuff can have been accomplished down through the millennia by wastrels, betrayers, and outcasts, and through people who were such complex mixtures of sinner and saint, and through so many obscure and undistinguished others, isn't that a pretty hopeful testament to the likelihood that God is using us, with our individual flaws and gifts, in all manner of peculiar and unexpected ways?

"Who of us can say we're not in the process of being used right now, this Advent, to fulfill some purpose whose grace and goodness would boggle our imagination if we could even begin to get our minds around it?

"Let me conclude my sermon with Father Brown, since he's been both the prod and mentor for it. He suggests that a thoughtful reflection on Matthew's genealogy encourages us during this liturgical season of Advent to continue the story of the sequence of Jesus Christ in this way: " 'Jesus called Peter and Paul...Paul called Timothy...someone called you... and you must call someone else'...Amen."

The Man Who Is God

Leonardo Boff

JESUS, A JEW OF NAZARETH; numbered among
the despised of Galilee (half of whose population was
pagan); juridically the son of the carpenter Joseph
and the virgin Mary, whose "sisters" and "brothers"
are known, e.g., Jacob, Joseph, Jude, and Simon
(Mark 6:3; Matt. 13:56); who was born under the
Roman Emperor Augustus in the *immensa romanae
pacis maiestas*, raised under Quirinius, governor of
the Province of Syria (Luke 2:1), and Pontius Pilate,
Roman administrator of Judea (Luke 3:1); and Herod
Antipas of Galilee (Luke 3:1), who was crucified under Emperor Tiberius on Friday, the fourteenth (according to John) or the fifteenth (according to the

Synoptics) of the month of Nisan, and a few days later rose again.

How does one understand that this concrete man, with his individual and datable history, is at one and the same time God? What greatness, sovereignty, and profundity must he not have revealed and lived in order to be called God? What does "God" mean now? What sort of human being is he, that we can make such an assertion about him? What does the unity of the two – God and man – concretely signify in a historical being, one of our brothers, Jesus of Nazareth?

This is one of the central facts of our faith that sets Christianity apart from other religions. Once Christianity affirms that a man is at the same time God, it stands alone in the world. We are obliged to say it: This is a scandal to the Jews and to all the religions and pious peoples of yesterday and today who venerate and adore a transcendent God: one that is totally other, who cannot be objectified, a God beyond this world, infinite, eternal, incomprehensible, and above everything that human beings can be and know. We Christians find that the God of the Jewish, pagan, and world religious experience has become concrete in a man, Jesus of Nazareth, in his life, words, and comportment, in his death and resurrection. We Christians learn the meaning of human persons, their roots and true humanity, by meditating on the human life of Jesus Christ.

However it is not by means of abstract analysis concerning the nature of God and human beings that we come to understand the nature of Jesus, the Man-God. Rather by seeing, imitating, and deciphering Jesus, by living together with him, we come to know God and human beings. The God who in and through Jesus reveals himself is human. And the human being who emerges in and through Jesus is divine. This is the specific characteristic of the Christian experience of God and human beings, one that is different from that of Judaism and paganism. It was in a man that the primitive church discovered God; and it was in God that we came to know the true nature and destiny of human beings.

The Light of the World

Evelyn Underhill

Now burn, new born to the world,
    Doubled-naturéd name,
The heaven-flung, heart-fleshed, maiden-furled
    Miracle-in-Mary-of-flame,
Mid-numbered He in three of the thunder-throne!
Not a dooms-day dazzle in his coming nor dark
       as he came;
    Kind, but royally reclaiming his own;
A released shower, let flash to the shire, not
       a lightning of fire hard-hurled.

GERARD MANLEY HOPKINS

WHEN WE COME to the first window at the east end
of the aisle, the morning light comes through it. It is

the window of the Incarnation. It brings us at once to the mingled homeliness and mystery of the Christian revelation and of our own little lives. It is full of family pictures and ideas – the birth of Christ, the Shepherds and the Magi, the little boy of Nazareth, the wonderful experience in the temple, the long quiet years in the carpenter's shop. There seems nothing so very supernatural about the first stage. But stand back and look – *Mira! Mira!*

We are being shown here something profoundly significant about human life – "God speaks in a Son," a baby son, and reverses all our pet values. He speaks in our language and shows us his secret beauty on our scale. We have got to begin not by an arrogant other-worldliness, but by a humble recognition that human things can be holy, very full of God, and that high-minded speculations about his nature need not be holy at all; that all life is engulfed in him and he can reach out to us anywhere at any level.

As the Christmas Day gospel takes us back to the mystery of the divine nature – *In the beginning was the Word...* – so let us begin by thinking of what St. Catherine called the "Ocean Pacific of the Godhead"

enveloping all life. The depth and richness of his being are entirely unknown to us, poor little scraps as
we are! And yet the unlimited life who is Love right
through – who loves and is wholly present where he
loves, on every plane and at every point – so loved
the world as to desire to give his essential thought,
the deepest secrets of his heart to this small, fugitive,
imperfect creation – to *us*. That seems immense.

And then the heavens open and what is dis-
closed? A baby, God manifest in the flesh. The
stable, the manger, the straw; poverty, cold, darkness – these form the setting of the divine gift. In
this child God gives his supreme message to the
soul – Spirit to spirit – but in a human way. Outside
in the fields the heavens open and the shepherds
look up astonished to find the music and radiance of
reality all around them. But inside, our closest contact with that same reality is being offered to us in
the very simplest, homeliest way – emerging right
into our ordinary life. A baby – just that. We are not
told that the blessed, virgin Mary saw the angels or
heard the *Gloria* in the air. Her initiation had been
quite different, like the quiet voice speaking in our

deepest prayer – "The Lord is with thee!" "Behold the handmaid of the Lord." Humble self-abandonment is quite enough to give us God.

Think of the tremendous contrast, transcendent and homely, brought together here as a clue to the Incarnation – the hard life of the poor, the absolute surrender and helplessness of babyhood and the unmeasured outpouring of divine life.

The Christmas mystery has two parts: the nativity and the epiphany. A deep instinct made the Church separate these two feasts. In the first we commemorate God's humble entrance into human life, the emergence and birth of the holy, and in the second its manifestation to the world, the revelation of the supernatural made in that life. And the two phases concern our inner lives very closely too. The first only happens in order that the second may happen, and the second cannot happen without the first. Christ is a Light to lighten the Gentiles as well as the glory of his people Israel. Think of what the Gentile was when these words were written – an absolute outsider. All cozy religious exclusiveness falls before that thought. The Light of the world is not the sanctuary lamp in your favorite church.

It is easy for the devout to join up with the shepherds and fall into place at the crib and look out into the surrounding night and say, "Look at those extraordinary intellectuals wandering about after a star, with no religious sense at all! Look at that clumsy camel, what an unspiritual animal it is! *We* know the ox and the ass are the right animals to have! Look what queer gifts and odd types of self-consecration they are bringing; not the sort of people who come to church!" But remember that the child who began by receiving these very unexpected pilgrims had a woman of the streets for his faithful friend and two thieves for his comrades at the end: and looking at these two extremes let us try to learn a little of the height and breadth and depth of his love – and then apply it to our own lives.

Beholding his glory is only half our job. In our souls too the mysteries must be brought forth; we are not really Christians till that has been done. "The Eternal Birth," says Eckhart, "must take place in *you*." And another mystic says human nature is like a stable inhabited by the ox of passion and the ass of prejudice; animals which take up a lot of room and which I suppose most of us are feeding on the quiet.

And it is there between them, pushing them out, that Christ must be born and in their very manger he must be laid – and they will be the first to fall on their knees before him. Sometimes Christians seem far nearer to those animals than to Christ in his simple poverty, self-abandoned to God.

The birth of Christ in our souls is for a purpose beyond ourselves: it is because his manifestation in the world must be through us. Every Christian is, as it were, part of the dust-laden air which shall radiate the glowing epiphany of God, catch and reflect his golden Light. *Ye are the light of the world* – but only because you are enkindled, made radiant by the one Light of the world. And being kindled, we have got to get on with it, be useful. As Christ said in one of his ironical flashes, "Do not light a candle in order to stick it under the bed!" Some people make a virtue of religious skulking.

When you don't see any startling marks of your own religious condition or your usefulness to God, think of the baby in the stable and the little Boy in the streets of Nazareth. The very life was there which was to change the whole history of the human race. There was not much to show for it. But there is entire continuity between the stable and the Easter garden and the thread that unites them is the will of God. The childlike simple prayer of Nazareth was the right preparation for the awful privilege of the Cross. Just so the light of the Spirit is to unfold gently and steadily within us, till at last our final stature, all God designed for us, is attained. It is an organic process, a continuous divine action, not a series of jerks. So on the one hand there should be no strain, impatience, self-willed effort in our prayer and self-discipline; and on the other, no settling down. A great flexibility, a gentle acceptance of what comes to us and a still gentler acceptance of the fact that much we see in others is still out of our reach. We must keep our prayer free, youthful – full of confidence and full of initiative too.

The mystics keep telling us that the goal of that prayer and the goal of that hidden life which should itself become more and more of a prayer, is "union with God." We use that phrase often, much too often to preserve the wholesome sense of its awe-fullness. For what does union with God mean? It is not a nice feeling we get in devout moments. That may or may not be a by-product of union – probably not. It can never be its substance. Union with God means every bit of our human nature transfigured in Christ, woven up into his creative life and activity, absorbed into his redeeming purpose, heart, soul, mind and strength. Each time it happens it means that one of God's creatures has achieved its destiny.

Room for Christ

Dorothy Day

IT IS NO USE SAYING that we are born two thousand years too late to give room to Christ. Nor will those who live at the end of the world have been born too late. Christ is always with us, always asking for room in our hearts.

But now it is with the voice of our contemporaries that he speaks, with the eyes of store clerks, factory workers, and children that he gazes; with the hands of office workers, slum dwellers, and suburban housewives that he gives. It is with the feet of soldiers and tramps that he walks, and with the heart of anyone in need that he longs for shelter. And giving shelter or food to anyone who asks for it, or needs it, is giving it to Christ.

We can do now what those who knew him in the days of his flesh did. I am sure that the shepherds did not adore and then go away to leave Mary and her Child in the stable, but somehow found them room, even though what they had to offer might have been primitive enough. All that the friends of Christ did for him in his lifetime, we can do. Peter's mother-in-law hastened to cook a meal for him, and if anything in the Gospels can be inferred, it surely is that she gave the very best she had, with no thought of extravagance. Matthew made a feast for him, inviting the whole town, so that the house was in an uproar of enjoyment, and the straitlaced Pharisees – the good people – were scandalized.

The people of Samaria, despised and isolated, were overjoyed to give him hospitality, and for days he walked and ate and slept among them. And the loveliest of all relationships in Christ's life, after his relationship with his Mother, is his friendship with Martha, Mary, and Lazarus and the continual hospitality he found with them. It is a staggering thought that there were once two sisters and a brother whom Jesus looked on almost as his family and where he found a second home, where Martha got on with her work, bustling around in her house-proud way, and Mary simply sat in silence with him.

If we hadn't got Christ's own words for it, it would seem raving lunacy to believe that if I offer a bed and food and hospitality to some man or woman or child, I am replaying the part of Lazarus or Martha or Mary, and that my guest is Christ. There is nothing to show it, perhaps. There are no halos already glowing round their heads – at least none that human eyes can see. It is not likely that I shall be vouchsafed the vision of Elizabeth of Hungary, who put the leper in her bed and later, going to tend him, saw no longer the leper's stricken face, but the face of Christ. The part of a Peter Claver, who gave a stricken Black man his bed and slept on the floor at his side, is more likely ours. For Peter Claver never saw anything with his bodily eyes except the exhausted faces of the Blacks; he had only faith in Christ's own words that these people were Christ. And when on one occasion the Blacks he had induced to help him ran from the room, panic-stricken before the disgusting sight of some sickness, he was astonished. "You mustn't go," he said, and you can still hear his surprise that anyone could forget such a truth: "You mustn't leave him – it is Christ."

Some time ago I saw the death notice of a sergeant-pilot who had been killed on active service. After the usual information, a message was added which, I imagine, is likely to be imitated. It said that anyone who had ever known the dead boy would always be sure of a welcome at his parents' home. So, even now that the war is over, the father and mother will go on taking in strangers for the simple reason that they will be reminded of their dead son by the friends he made.

That is rather like the custom that existed among the first generations of Christians, when faith was a bright fire that warmed more than those who kept it burning. In every house then, a room was kept ready for any stranger who might ask for shelter; it was even called "the stranger's room"; and this not because these people, like the parents of the dead airman, thought they could trace something of someone they loved in the stranger who used it, not because the man or woman to whom they gave shelter reminded them of Christ, but because – plain and simple and stupendous fact – he *was* Christ.

It would be foolish to pretend that it is always easy to remember this. If everyone were holy and handsome, with *alter Christus* shining in neon lighting from them, it would be easy to see Christ in everyone. If Mary had appeared in Bethlehem clothed, as St. John says, with the sun, a crown of twelve stars on her head, and the moon under her feet, then people would have fought to make room for her. But that was not God's way for her, nor is it Christ's way for himself, now when he is disguised under every type of humanity that treads the earth.

To see how far one realizes this, it is a good thing to ask honestly what you would do, or have done, when a beggar asked at your house for food. Would you – or did you – give it on an old cracked plate, thinking that was good enough? Do you think that Martha and Mary thought that the old and chipped dish was good enough for their guest?

In Christ's human life, there were always a few who made up for the neglect of the crowd. The shepherds did it; their hurrying to the crib atoned for the people who would flee from Christ. The wise men did it; their journey across the world made up for those who refused to stir one hand's breadth from the routine of their lives to go to Christ. Even the gifts the wise men brought have in themselves an obscure recompense and atonement for what would follow later in this Child's life. For they brought gold, the king's emblem, to make up for the crown of thorns that he would wear; they offered incense, the symbol of praise, to make up for the mockery and the spitting; they gave him myrrh, to heal and soothe, and he was wounded from head to foot and no one bathed his wounds. The women at the foot of the Cross did it too, making up for the crowd who stood by and sneered.

We can do it too, exactly as they did. We are not born too late. We do it by seeing Christ and serving Christ in friends and strangers, in everyone we come in contact with.

All this can be proved, if proof is needed, by the doctrines of the Church. We can talk about Christ's Mystical Body, about the vine and the branches, about the Communion of Saints. But Christ himself has proved it for us, and no one has to go further than that. For he said that a glass of water given to a beggar was given to him. He made heaven hinge on the way we act toward him in his disguise of commonplace, frail, ordinary humanity.

Did you give me food when I was hungry?

Did you give me to drink when I was thirsty?

Did you give me clothes when my own were rags?

Did you come to see me when I was sick, or in prison or in trouble?

And to those who say, aghast, that they never had a chance to do such a thing, that they lived two thousand years too late, he will say again what they had the chance of knowing all their lives, that if these things were done for the very least of his brethren they were done to him.

For a total Christian, the goad of duty is not needed – always prodding one to perform this or that good deed. It is not a duty to help Christ, it is a privilege. Is it likely that Martha and Mary sat back and considered that they had done all that was expected of them – is it likely that Peter's mother-in-law grudgingly served the chicken she had meant to keep till Sunday because she thought it was her "duty"? She did it gladly; she would have served ten chickens if she had had them.

If that is the way they gave hospitality to Christ, then certainly it is the way it should still be given. Not for the sake of humanity. Not because it might be Christ who stays with us, comes to see us, takes up our time. Not because these people remind us of Christ, as those soldiers and airmen remind the parents of their son, but because they *are* Christ, asking us to find room for him, exactly as he did at the first Christmas.

Shipwrecked
at the Stable

Brennan Manning

DO YOU THINK you could contain Niagara Falls in a teacup?

Is there anyone in our midst who pretends to understand the awesome love in the heart of the Abba of Jesus that inspired, motivated and brought about Christmas? The shipwrecked at the stable kneel in the presence of mystery.

God entered into our world not with the crushing impact of unbearable glory, but in the way of weakness, vulnerability and need. On a wintry night in an obscure cave, the infant Jesus was a humble, naked, helpless God who allowed us to get close to him.

We all know how difficult it is to receive anything from someone who has all the answers, who is completely cool, utterly unafraid, needing nothing and in control of every situation. We feel unnecessary, unrelated to this paragon. So God comes as a newborn baby, giving us a chance to love him, making us feel that we have something to give him.

The world does not understand vulnerability. Neediness is rejected as incompetence and compassion is dismissed as unprofitable. The great deception of television advertising is that being poor, vulnerable and weak is unattractive. A fat monk named "Brother Dominic" is cute and cool because he conquers vulnerability and helplessness by buying into the competitive world with a Xerox machine.

The spirituality of Bethlehem is simply incomprehensible to the advertising industry. The opening notes of Beethoven's Fifth Symphony are being used to sell us pain reliever, and the prayer of St. Francis is being used to sell us hair conditioner.

The Bethlehem mystery will ever be a scandal to aspiring disciples who seek a triumphant Savior and a prosperity Gospel. The infant Jesus was born in unimpressive circumstances, no one can exactly say where. His parents were of no social significance whatsoever, and his chosen welcoming committee were all turkeys, losers and dirt-poor shepherds. But in this weakness and poverty the shipwrecked at the stable would come to know the love of God.

Sadly, Christian piety down through the centuries has prettified the Babe of Bethlehem. Christian art has trivialized divine scandal into gingerbread crèches. Christian worship has sentimentalized the smells of the stable into dignified pageant...

Pious imagination and nostalgic music rob Christmas of its shock value, while some scholars reduce the crib to a tame theological symbol. But the shipwrecked at the stable tremble in adoration of the Christ-child and quake at the inbreak of God Almighty. Because all the Santa Clauses and red-nosed reindeer, fifty-foot trees and thundering church bells put together create less pandemonium than the infant Jesus when, instead of remaining a statue in a crib, he comes alive and delivers us over to the fire that he came to light.

The Spanish author José Ortega puts it this way:

The man with the clear head is the man who frees himself from fantasy and looks life in the face, realizes that everything in it is problematic, and feels himself lost. And this is the simple truth – that to live is to feel oneself lost. Whoever accepts this has already begun to find himself, to be on firm ground. *Instinctively, as do the shipwrecked*, he will look around for something to which to cling, and that tragic, ruthless glance, absolutely sincere because it is a question of his salvation, will cause him to bring order to the chaos of his life. *These are the only genuine ideas; the ideas of the shipwrecked.* All the rest is rhetoric, posturing, farce. He who does not really feel himself lost, is without remission; that is to say, he never finds himself, never comes up against his own reality.

The shipwrecked at the stable are the poor in spirit who feel lost in the cosmos, adrift on an open sea, clinging with a life-and-death desperation to the one solitary plank. Finally they are washed ashore and make their way to the stable, stripped of the old spirit of possessiveness in regard to anything. The shipwrecked find it not only tacky but utterly absurd to be caught up either in tinsel trees or in religious experiences – "Doesn't going to church on Christmas make you feel good?" They are not concerned with their own emotional security or any of the trinkets of creation. They have been saved, rescued, de-livered from the waters of death, set free for a new shot at life. At the stable in a blinding moment of truth, they make the stunning discovery that Jesus is the plank of salvation they have been clinging to without knowing it!

All the time they were battered by wind and rain, buffeted by raging seas, they were being held even when they didn't know who was holding them. Their exposure to spiritual, emotional and physical deprivation has weaned them from themselves and made them re-examine all they once thought impor-tant. The shipwrecked come to the stable seeking not to possess but to be possessed, wanting not peace or a religious high, but Jesus Christ.

The shipwrecked don't seek peace because they aren't disturbed by the lack of it. By that I mean the subjective feeling of peace. Circumstances can play havoc with our emotions, the day can be stormy or fair and our feelings will fluctuate accordingly; but if we are in Christ Jesus, we are in peace and there unflustered *even when we feel no peace*. Meister Eckhart's equation, "In Christ equals in peace," is al-ways valid. When we accept the truth of ourselves –

shipwrecked and saved – our lives are henceforth anchored in the Rock who is Christ, not in the shifting sands of our fickle feelings.

This is a point of capital importance for those who would fully experience the grace of Christmas. When we are in right relationship with Jesus, we are in the peace of Christ. Except for grave, conscious, deliberate infidelity, which must be recognized and repented of, the presence or absence of *feelings* of peace is the normal ebb and flow of the spiritual life. When things are plain and ordinary, when we live on the plateaus and in the valleys (which is where most of the Christian life takes place) and not on the mountaintops of peak religious experiences, this is no reason to blame ourselves, to think that our relationship with God is collapsing, or to echo Magdalene's cry in the garden, "Where has my beloved gone?" Frustration, irritation, fatigue and so forth may temporarily unsettle us, but they cannot rob us of living in the peace of Christ Jesus. As the playwright Ionesco once declared in the middle of a depression: "Nothing discourages me, not even discouragement."

The shipwrecked have stood at the still-point of a turning world and discovered that the human heart is made for Jesus Christ and cannot really be content with less. They cannot take seriously the demands that the world makes on them. During Advent they teach us that the more we try to tame and reduce desires, the more we deceive and distort ourselves. We are made for Christ and nothing less will ever satisfy us. As Paul writes in Colossians 1:16, "All things were created by him and for him." And further on, "There is only Christ: he is everything" (3:11). It is only in Christ that the heart finds true joy in created things.

To the clotheshorse fretting about what to wear on Christmas Day, the shipwrecked say, "Put on Christ." To the merchant whose Bible is the *Wall Street Journal* and who pants down the money-making street, the shipwrecked say, "You have only one Master; serving him is incompatible with any other servitude." To the power-broker dealing strength to get things done, the shipwrecked say: "However powerful you are, the most you can do is change the décor of a world that is collapsing into its own death."

The shipwrecked stand on firm ground. They live in truth and are rooted in reality. They do not allow the world to order them around. Kneeling at the crib they find the vanity of the world ridiculous, bloated, preposterous...

Do you hear what the shipwrecked are saying? Let go of your paltry desires and expand your expectations. Christmas means that God has given us nothing less than himself and his name is Jesus Christ. Be unwilling next Christmas to settle for anything else. Don't order "just a piece of toast" when eggs Benedict are on the menu. Don't come with a thimble when God has nothing less to give you than the ocean of himself. Don't be contented with a "nice" Christmas when Jesus says, "It has pleased my Father to give you the Kingdom." Pray, go to work, play Trivial Pursuit, eat banana bread, exchange presents, go caroling, feed the hungry, comfort the lonely, and do all in the name of our Lord Jesus Christ.

There is a beautiful story recounted every Christmas in the forests of Provence in southern France. It's about the four shepherds who came to Bethlehem to see the child. One brought eggs, another bread and cheese, the third brought wine. And the fourth brought nothing at all. People called him *L'Enchanté*. The first three shepherds chatted with Mary and Joseph, commenting on how well Mary looked, how cozy was the cave and how handsomely Joseph had appointed it, what a beautiful starlit night it was. They congratulated the proud parents, presented them with their gifts and assured them that if they needed anything else, they had only to ask. Finally someone asked, "Where is *L'Enchanté?*" They searched high and low, up and down, inside and out. Finally, someone peeked through the blanket hung against the draft, into the creche. There, kneeling at the crib, was *L'Enchanté* – the Enchanted One. Like a flag or a flame taking the direction of the wind, he had taken the direction of love. Throughout the entire night, he stayed in adoration, whispering, "Jesu, Jesu, Jesu – Jesus, Jesus, Jesus."

As Christmas approaches, an honest question is: do I want to be or merely *appear* to be a Christian? Like the shipwrecked, the Enchanted One is laid waste by one pure passion. His singlemindedness leads him to a realistic assessment: anything connected with Christmas that is not centered in Christ Jesus – tree, ornaments, turkey dinner, exchange of gifts, worship itself – is empty gesturing. Blessed are the shipwrecked, for they see God in all the trappings of Christmas and experience a joy that the world does not understand.

One day Saint Francis and Brother Leo were walking down the road. Noticing that Leo was depressed, Francis turned and asked: "Leo, do you know what it means to be pure of heart?"

"Of course. It means to have no sins, faults or weaknesses to reproach myself for."

"Ah," said Francis, "now I understand why you're sad. We will always have something to reproach ourselves for."

"Right," said Leo. "That's why I despair of ever arriving at purity of heart."

"Leo, listen carefully to me. Don't be so preoccupied with the purity of your heart. Turn and look at Jesus. Admire him. Rejoice that he is what he is – your Brother, your Friend, your Lord and Savior. That, little brother, is what it means to be pure of heart. And once you've turned to Jesus, don't turn back and look at yourself. Don't wonder where you stand with him.

"The sadness of not being perfect, the discovery that you really are sinful, is a feeling much too human, even borders on idolatry. Focus your vision outside yourself on the beauty, graciousness and compassion of Jesus Christ. The pure of heart praise him from sunrise to sundown. Even when they feel broken, feeble, distracted, insecure and uncertain, they are able to release it into his peace. A heart like that is stripped and filled – stripped of self and filled with the fullness of God. It is enough that Jesus is Lord."

After a long pause, Leo said, "Still, Francis, the Lord demands our effort and fidelity."

"No doubt about that," replied Francis. "But holiness is not a personal achievement. It's an emptiness you discover in yourself. Instead of resenting it, you accept it and it becomes the free space where the Lord can create anew. To cry out, 'You alone are the Holy One, you alone are the Lord,' that is what it means to be pure of heart. And it doesn't come by your Herculean efforts and threadbare resolutions."

"Then how?" asked Leo.

"Simply hoard nothing of yourself; sweep the house clean. Sweep out even the attic, even the nagging painful consciousness of your past. Accept being shipwrecked. Renounce everything that is heavy, even the weight of your sins. See only the compassion, the infinite patience, and the tender love of Christ. Jesus is Lord. That suffices. Your guilt and reproach disappear into the nothingness of non-attention. You are no longer aware of yourself, like the sparrow aloft and free in the azure sky. Even the desire for holiness is transformed into a pure and simple desire for Jesus."

Leo listened gravely as he walked along beside Francis. Step by step he felt his heart grow lighter as a profound peace flooded his soul. The shipwrecked have little in common with the landlocked. The landlocked have their own security system, a home base, credentials and credit cards, storehouses and barns, their self-interest and investments intact. They never find themselves because they never re-ally feel themselves lost. At Christmas, one despairs of finding a suitable gift for the landlocked. "They're so hard to shop for; they have everything they need."

The shipwrecked, on the contrary, reach out for that passing plank with the desperation of the drowning. Adrift on an angry sea, in a state of utter helplessness and vulnerability, the shipwrecked never asked what they could *do* to merit the plank and inherit the kingdom of dry land. They knew that there was absolutely nothing any of them could do. Like little children, they simply *received* the plank as a gift. And little children are precisely those who haven't done anything. "Unless you…become like little children, you will never enter the kingdom of heaven" (Matt. 18:3). Jesus is not suggesting that heaven is a vast playground for infants. Children are our model because they have no claim of heaven. If they are close to God, Simon Tugwell says, "it is not because they are innocent, but because they are incompetent…"

When Jesus tells us to become like little children, he is urging us to forget what lies behind. Children have no past. Whatever we have done in the past, be it good or evil, great or small, it is irrelevant to our stance before Jesus. It is only now that we are in his presence, and this Christmas is the First Christmas of the rest of our lives. Like little children, the shipwrecked don't bring the baggage of the past into the stable of the present moment…

The shipwrecked at the stable are captivated by joy and wonder. They have found the treasure in the field of Bethlehem. The pearl of great price is wrapped in swaddling clothes and lying in a manger. Everything else is cheap, fake, painted fragments of glass.

The question for all of us is what we will really aim at next Christmas. If all we are going for is a placid decency, routine prayer, well-behaved worship and comfortable compassion, then we have effectively parted company with the shipwrecked and have no fellowship with the pearl-finder.

I wonder, if we were to stop people at random in the street on December 24 and ask them what they want most for Christmas, how many would say, "I want to see Jesus"?

I believe that the single most important consideration during the sacred season of Advent is *intensity of desire*. Paraphrasing the late Rabbi Abraham Heschel, "Jesus Christ is of no importance unless he is of supreme importance." An intense inner desire is already the sign of his presence in our hearts. The rest is the work of the Holy Spirit.

Perhaps many of us are in the same position as the Greeks in chapter twelve of John's Gospel who approached Philip and said, "We would like to see Jesus."

The question addressed to each of us is: How badly?

The shipwrecked at the stable are an indispensable presence in the church. They rescue the Savior from the snare of convention and the clutches of organized religion. They are marginal men and women, not leaders or decision-makers. In their ministry of quiet presence they do not need to win or compete. They may look like losers even to themselves. If they courted the world, the world might respect them; if they rejected the world in sullen disdain, it might respect them even more. But because they take no notice at all of what the world thinks of them, they are mocked and made fun of.

The only explanation of why the little band of the shipwrecked exists at all is the personal magnetism of Jesus. As Bernard of Clairvaux wrote, "Only he who has experienced it can believe what the love of Jesus Christ is." You could more easily catch a hurricane in a shrimp net than you can understand the wild, relentless, passionate, uncompromising, pursuing love of God made present in the manger.

In 1980, the day before Christmas, Richard Ballenger's mother in Anderson, South Carolina, was busy wrapping packages and asked her young son to shine her shoes. Soon, with the proud smile that only a seven-year-old can muster, he presented the shoes for inspection. His mother was so pleased, she gave him a quarter.

On Christmas morning as she put on the shoes to go to church, she noticed a lump in one shoe. She took it off and found a quarter wrapped in paper. Written on the paper in a child's scrawl were the words, "I done it for love."

When the final curtain falls, each of us will be the sum of our choices throughout life, the sum of the appointments we kept and the appointments we didn't keep. The glory of the shipwrecked will be that they habitually failed to turn up for duty. In their defense they claim they were detained by a baby in swaddling clothes. When interrogated as to why they hung out at a stable, they answer, "We done it for love."

In their integrity the shipwrecked preserve the meaning of Christmas in its pristine purity – the birthday of the Savior and the eruption of the messianic era into history.

This Christmas, may you belong to their number.

The Coming of Jesus in Our Midst

Dietrich Bonhoeffer

Behold, I stand at the door and knock; if anyone hears my voice and opens the door, I will come in to him and eat with him, and he with me.

REVELATION 3:20

WHEN EARLY CHRISTIANITY SPOKE of the return of the Lord Jesus, they thought of a great day of judgment. Even though this thought may appear to us to be so unlike Christmas, it is original Christianity and to be taken extremely seriously. When we hear Jesus knocking, our conscience first of all pricks us: Are we rightly prepared? Is our heart capable of becoming God's dwelling place? Thus Advent becomes a time of self-examination. "Put the desires of your heart in order, O human beings!" (Valentin Thilo), as the old song sings. It is very remarkable that we face the thought that God is coming so calmly, whereas previously peoples trembled at the day of God, whereas the world fell into trembling when Jesus Christ walked over the earth. That is why we find it so strange when we see the marks of God in the world so often together with the marks of human suffering, with the marks of the cross on Golgotha. We have become so accustomed to the idea of divine love and of God's coming at Christmas that we no longer feel the shiver of fear that God's coming should arouse in us. We are indifferent to the message, taking only the pleasant and agreeable out of it and forgetting the serious aspect, that the God of the world draws near to the people of our little earth and lays claim to us. The coming of God is truly not only glad tidings, but first of all frightening news for everyone who has a conscience.

Only when we have felt the terror of the matter, can we recognize the incomparable kindness. God comes into the very midst of evil and of death, and judges the evil in us and in the world. And by judging us, God cleanses and sanctifies us, comes to us with grace and love. God makes us happy as only children can be happy. God wants to always be with us, wherever we may be – in our sin, in our suffering and death. We are no longer alone; God is with us. We are no longer homeless; a bit of the eternal home itself has moved unto us. Therefore we adults can rejoice deeply within our hearts under the Christmas tree, perhaps much more than the children are able. We know that God's goodness will once again draw near. We think of all of God's goodness that came our way last year and sense something of this marvelous home. Jesus comes in judgment and grace: "Behold I stand at the door...Open wide the gates!" (Ps. 24:7)...

One day, at the last judgment, he will separate the sheep and the goats and will say to those on his right: "Come, you blessed... I was hungry and you fed me..." (Matt. 25:34). To the astonished question of when and where, he answered: "What you did to the least of these, you have done to me..." (Matt. 25:40). With that we are faced with the shocking reality: Jesus stands at the door and knocks, in complete reality. He asks you for help in the form of a beggar, in the form of a ruined human being in torn clothing. He confronts you in every person that you meet. Christ walks on the earth as your neighbor as long as there are people. He walks on the earth as the one through whom God calls you, speaks to you and makes his demands. That is the greatest seriousness and the greatest blessedness of the Advent message. Christ stands at the door. He lives in the form of the person in our midst. Will you keep the door locked or open it to him?

Christ is still knocking. It is not yet Christmas. But it is also not the great final Advent, the final coming of Christ. Through all the Advents of our life that we celebrate goes the longing for the final Advent, where it says: "Behold, I make all things new" (Rev. 21:5). Advent is a time of waiting. Our whole life, however, is Advent – that is, a time of waiting for the ultimate, for the time when there will be a new heaven and a new earth, when all people are brothers and sisters and one rejoices in the words of the angels: "On earth peace to those on whom God's favor rests." Learn to wait, because he has promised to come. "I stand at the door…" We however call to him: "Yes, come soon, Lord Jesus!" Amen.

The Holy Mother

Romano Guardini

*"How will this be," Mary asked the angel, "since I am a vir-
gin?" The angel answered, "The Holy Spirit will come upon
you, and the power of the Most High will overshadow you. So
the Holy One to be born will be called the Son of God...For
nothing is impossible with God."*

*"I am the Lord's servant," Mary answered. "May it be
with me as you have said." Then the angel left her.*

LUKE 1:34–38

ANYONE WHO WOULD UNDERSTAND the nature
of a tree should examine the earth that encloses its
roots, the soil from which its sap climbs into branch,
blossom, and fruit. Similarly to understand the person of Jesus Christ, one would do well to look to the
soil that brought him forth: Mary, his mother.

We are told that she was of royal descent. Mary's response to the message of the angel was queenly. In that moment she was confronted with something of unprecedented magnitude, something that exacted a trust in God reaching into a darkness far beyond human comprehension. And she gave her answer simply, utterly unconscious of the greatness of her act. A large measure of that greatness was certainly the heritage of her blood.

From that instant until her death, Mary's destiny was shaped by that of her child. This is soon evident in the grief that steps between herself and her betrothed; in the journey to Bethlehem; the birth in danger and poverty; the sudden break from the protection of her home and the flight to a strange country with all the rigors of exile – until at last she is permitted to return to Nazareth.

It is not until much later – when her twelve-year-old son remains behind in the temple, to be found after an agony of seeking – that the divine "otherness" of that which stands at the center of her existence is revealed (Luke 2:41–50). To the certainly understandable reproach: "Son, why hast thou done so to us? Behold, in sorrow thy father and I have been seeking thee," the boy replies, "How is it that you sought me? Did you not know that I must be about my Father's business?" In that hour Mary must have begun to comprehend Simeon's prophecy: "And thy own soul a sword shall pierce" (Luke 2:35). For what but the sword of God can it mean when a child in such a moment answers his disturbed mother with an amazed: "How is it that you sought me"? We are not surprised to read further down the page: "And they did not understand the word that he spoke to them." Then directly: "And his mother kept all these things carefully in her heart." Not understanding, she buries the words like precious seed within her. The incident is typical: the mother's vision is unequal to that of her son, but her heart, like chosen ground, is deep enough to sustain the highest tree.

Eighteen years of silence follow. Not a word in the sacred records, save that the boy "went down with them" and "advanced" in wisdom, years, and grace "before God and men." Eighteen years of silence passing through this heart – yet to the attentive ear, the silence of the gospels speaks powerfully. Deep, still eventfulness enveloped in the silent love of this holiest of mothers.

Then Jesus leaves his home to shoulder his mission. Still Mary is near him; at the wedding feast at Cana, for instance, with its last gesture of maternal direction and care (John 2:1–11). Later, disturbed by wild rumors circulating in Nazareth, she leaves everything and goes to him, stands fearfully outside the door (Mark 3:21, 31–35). And at the last she is with him, under the cross to the end (John 19:25).

From the first hour to the last, Jesus' life is enfolded in the nearness of his mother. The strongest part of their relationship is her silence. Nevertheless, if we accept the words Jesus speaks to her simply as they arise from each situation, it seems almost invariably as if a cleft gaped between him and her. Take the incident in the temple of Jerusalem. He was, after all, only a child when he stayed behind without a word, at a time when the city was overflowing with pilgrims of all nationalities, and when not only accidents but every kind of violence was to be expected. Surely they had a right to ask why he had acted as he did. Yet his reply expresses only amazement. No wonder they failed to understand!

It is the same with the wedding feast at Cana in Galilee. He is seated at table with the wedding party, apparently poor people, who haven't much to offer. They run out of wine, and everyone feels the growing embarrassment. Pleadingly, Mary turns to her son: "They have no wine."

But he replies only: "What wouldst thou have me do, woman? My hour has not yet come." In other words, I must wait for my hour; from minute to minute I must obey the voice of my Father – no other. Directly he does save the situation, but only because suddenly (the unexpected, often instantaneous manner in which God's commands are made known to the prophets may help us to grasp what happens here) his hour *has* come (John 2:1–11). Another time, Mary comes down from Galilee to see him: "Behold, thy mother and thy brethren are outside, seeking thee." He answers, "Who are my mother and my brethren? Whoever does the will of God, he is my brother and sister and mother" (Mark 3:32–35). And though certainly he goes out to her and receives her with love, the words remain, and we feel the shock of his reply and sense something of the unspeakable remoteness in which he lived.

Even his reply to the words "Blessed is the womb that bore thee," sometimes interpreted as an expression of nearness, could also mean distance: "Rather, blessed are they who hear the word of God and keep it."

Finally on Calvary, his mother under the cross, thirsting for a word, her heart crucified with him, he says with a glance at John: "Woman, behold, thy son." And to John: "Behold, thy mother" (John 19:26–27). Expression, certainly, of a dying son's solicitude for his mother's future, yet her heart must have twinged. Once again she is directed away from him. Christ must face the fullness of his ultimate hour, huge, terrible, all-demanding, alone; must fulfill it from the reaches of extreme isolation, utterly alone with the load of sin that he has shouldered, before the justice of God.

Everything that affected Jesus affected his mother, yet no intimate understanding existed between them. His life was hers, yet constantly escaped her. Scripture puts it clearly: he is "the Holy One" promised by the angel, a title full of the mystery and remoteness of God. Mary gave that holy burden everything: heart, honor, flesh and blood, all the wonderful strength of her love. In the beginning she had contained it, but soon it outgrew her, mounting steadily higher and higher to the world of the divine beyond her reach.

Here he had lived, far removed from her. Certainly, Mary did not comprehend the ultimate. How could she, a mortal, fathom the mystery of the living God! But she was capable of something which on earth is more than understanding, something possible only through that same divine power which, when the hour has come, grants understanding: faith. She believed, and at a time when in the fullest sense of the word probably no one believed. "And blessed is she who has believed..." If anything voices Mary's greatness, it is this cry of her cousin Elizabeth.

Mary believed blindly. Again and again she had to confirm that belief, and each time with more difficulty. Her faith was greater, more heroic than that of any other human being. Involuntarily we call to mind Abraham and the sudden, terrible sublimity of his faith; but more was demanded of Mary than Abraham. For years she had to combat an only too natural confusion. Who was this "Holy One" whom she, a mere girl, had borne? This "great" one she had suckled and known in all his helplessness? Later she had to struggle against the pain of seeing him steadily outgrow her love, even purposely flee it to that realm of ineffable remoteness which she could not enter. Not only did she have to accept this, but to rejoice in it as in the fulfillment of God's will. Not understanding, never was she to lose heart, never to fall behind. Inwardly she accompanied the incomprehensible figure of her son every step of his journey, however dark. Perseverance in faith, even on Calvary – this was Mary's inimitable greatness.

And literally, every step the Lord took towards fulfillment of his godly destiny Mary followed – in bare faith. Comprehension came only with Pentecost. Then she understood all that she had so long reverently stored in her heart. It is this heroic faith which places her irrevocably at Christ's side in the work of redemption, not the miracles of Marianic legend. What is demanded of us, as of her, is a constant wrestling *in fide* with the mystery of God and with the evil resistance of the world. Our obligation is not delightful poetry but granite faith.

Mary's vital depths supported the Lord throughout his life and death. Again and again he left her behind to feel the blade of the "sword" – but each time, in a surge of faith, she caught up with him and enfolded him anew, until at last he severed the very bond of sonship, appointing another, the man beside her under the cross, to take his place! On the highest, thinnest pinnacle of creation Jesus stood alone, face to face with the justice of God. From the depths of her co-agony on Golgotha, Mary, with a final bound of faith, accepted this double separation – and once again stood beside him! Indeed, "Blessed is she who has believed!"

Bethlehem

Annie Dillard

ONE OF THE QUEEREST spots on earth – I hope –
is the patch of planet where, according to tradition,
a cave once stabled animals, and where Mary gave
birth to a son whose later preaching – scholars of
every stripe agree, with varying enthusiasm – caused
the occupying Romans to crucify him. Generations
of Christians have churched over the traditional
Bethlehem spot to the highest degree. Centuries of
additions have made the architecture peculiar, but
no one can see the church anyway, because many
monasteries clamp onto it in clusters like barnacles.
The Greek Orthodox Church owns the grotto site
now, in the form of the Church of the Nativity.

There, in the Church of the Nativity, I took worn stone stairways to descend to levels of dark rooms, chapels, and dungeonlike corridors where hushed people passed. The floors were black stone or cracked marble. Dense brocades hung down old stone walls. Oil lamps hung in layers. Each polished silver or brass lamp seemed to absorb more light than its orange flame emitted, so the more lamps shone, the darker the space.

Packed into a tiny, domed upper chamber, Norwegians sang, as every other group did in turn, a Christmas carol. The stone dome bounced the sound around. The people sounded like seraphs singing inside a bell, sore amazed.

Descending once more, I passed several monks, narrow men, fine-faced and black, who wore tall black hats and long black robes. Ethiopians, they use the oldest Christian rite. At a lower level, in a small room, I peered over half a stone wall and saw Europeans below; they whispered in a language I could not identify.

Distant music sounded deep, as if from within my ribs. The music was, in fact, people from all over the world in the upper chamber, singing harmonies in their various tongues. The music threaded the vaults.

Now I climbed down innumerable dark stone stairs to the main part, the deepest basement: The Grotto of the Nativity. The grotto was down yet another smoky stairway, at the back of a stone cave far beneath street level. This was the place. It smelled of wet sand. It was a narrow cave about ten feet wide; cracked marble paved it. Bunched tapers, bending grotesque in the heat, lighted a corner of floor. People had to kneel, one by one, under arches of brocade hangings, and stretch into a crouch down among dozens of gaudy hanging lamps, to see it.

A fourteen-pointed silver star, two feet in diameter, covered a raised bit of marble floor at the cave wall. This silver star was the X that marked the spot: Here, just here, the infant got born. Two thousand years of Christianity began here, where God emptied himself into man. Actually, many Christian scholars think "Jesus of Nazareth" was likely born in Nazareth. Early writers hooked his birth to Bethlehem to fit a prophecy. Here, now, the burning oils smelled heavy. It must have struck many people that we were competing with these lamps for oxygen.

In the center of the silver star was a circular hole. That was the bull's eye, God's quondam target.

Crouching people leaned forward to wipe their fingers across the hole's flat bottom. When it was my turn, I knelt, bent under a fringed satin drape, reached across half the silver star, and touched its hole. I could feel some sort of soft wax in it. The hole was a quarter inch deep and six inches across, like a wide petri dish. I have never read any theologian who claims that God is particularly interested in religion, anyway.

Any patch of ground anywhere smacks more of God's presence on earth, to me, than did this marble grotto. The ugliness of the blunt and bumpy silver star impressed me. The bathetic pomp of the heavy, tasseled brocades, the marble, the censers hanging from chains, the embroidered antependium, the aspergillum, the crosiers, the ornate lamps – some human's idea of elegance – bespoke grand comedy, too, that God put up with it. And why should he not? Things here on earth get a whole lot worse than bad taste.

"Every day," said Rabbi Nachman of Bratslav, "the glory is ready to emerge from its debasement."

To *You* Christ Is Born

Martin Luther

The angel said to them, "Behold, I bring you good tidings of great joy which shall be to all the people; for there is born to you this day a Savior, who is Christ the Lord."

THE GOSPEL TEACHES THAT Christ was born, and that he died and suffered everything on our behalf, as is here declared by the angel. In these words you clearly see that he is born for us.

He does not simply say, Christ is born, but to *you* he is born. Neither does he say, I bring glad tidings, but to *you* I bring glad tidings of great joy. Furthermore, this joy was not to remain in Christ, but it shall be to all the people. This faith no condemned or wicked man has, nor can he have it. Christ has a pure, innocent, and holy birth. Man has an unclean, sinful, condemned birth; as David says (Psalms 51:5): "Behold, I was brought forth in iniquity; and in sin did my mother conceive me." Nothing can help this unholy birth except the pure birth of Christ. For this purpose Christ willed to be born, that through him we might be born anew.

O, this is the great joy of which the angel speaks. This is the comfort and exceeding goodness of God that, if anyone believes this, he can boast of the treasure that Mary is his rightful mother, Christ his brother, and God his father. For these things actually occurred and are true, but we must believe. This is the principal thing and the principal treasure in every Gospel. Christ must above all things become our own and we become his. This is what is meant by Isaiah 9:6: "Unto us a child is born, unto us a son is given." To *you* is born and given this child.

Therefore see to it that you do not treat the Gospel only as history, for that is only transient; neither regard it only as an example, for it is of no value without faith. Rather, see to it that you make this birth your own and that Christ be born in you. This will be the case if you believe, then you will repose in the lap of the virgin Mary and be her dear child. But you must exercise this faith and pray while you live; you cannot establish it too firmly. This is our foundation and inheritance, upon which good works must be built.

The Gospel does not merely teach about the history of Christ. No, it enables all who believe it to receive it as their own, which is the way the Gospel operates. Of what benefit would it be to me if Christ had been born a thousand times, and it would daily be sung into my ears in a most lovely manner, if I were never to hear that he was born for me and was to be my very own? If the voice gives forth this pleasant sound, even if it be in homely phrase, my heart listens with joy, for it is a lovely sound which penetrates the soul.

If Christ has indeed become your own, and you have by such faith been cleansed through him and have received your inheritance without any personal merit, it follows that you will do good works by doing to your neighbor as Christ has done to you. Here good works are their own teacher. What are the good works of Christ? Is it not true that they are good because they have been done for your benefit, for God's sake, who commanded him to do the works in your behalf? In this then Christ was obedient to the Father, in that he loved and served us.

Therefore since you have received enough and become rich, you have no other commandment than to serve Christ and render obedience to him. Direct your works that they may be of benefit to your neighbor, just as the works of Christ are of benefit to you. For this reason Jesus said at the Last Supper: "This is my commandment, that you love one another; even as I have loved you." Here it is seen that he loved us and did everything for our benefit, in order that we may do the same, not to him, for he needs it not, but to our neighbor. This is his commandment, and this is our obedience. Christ helps us, so we in return help our neighbor, and all have enough.

Notice then how far off those are who expend their energies uniting good works with stone. Of what benefit is it to your neighbor if you build a church entirely out of gold? Of what benefit to him is the frequent ringing of great church bells? Of what benefit to him is the glitter and the ceremonies in the churches, the clergy's robes, the sanctuary? Of what benefit to him are the many candles or the singing of vigils and liturgies? Do you think that God wants to be served with the sound of bells, the smoke of candles and such fancies? He has commanded none of these, but if you see your neighbor going astray, sinning, or suffering in body or soul, you are to leave every thing else and at once help him in every way in your power and if you can do no more, help him with words of comfort and prayer. Thus has Christ done to you and given you an example for you to follow.

Here Jesus does what he says: "And the poor have good tidings preached to them," and "Blessed are the poor in spirit; for theirs is the kingdom of heaven" (Mt. 11:5; 5:8). Here are no learned, no rich, no mighty ones, for such people do not as a rule accept the Gospel. The Gospel is a heavenly treasure, which will not tolerate any other treasure, and will not agree with any earthly guest in the heart. Therefore whoever loves the one must let go the other, as Christ says, "You cannot serve God and mammon" (Mt. 6:24).

This is shown by the shepherds in that they were in the field, under the canopy of heaven, and not in houses, showing that they do not hold fast and cling to temporal things. And besides being in the fields by night, they are despised by and unknown to the world which sleeps in the night, and by day delights so to walk that it may be noticed; but the poor shepherds go about their work at night. They represent all the lowly who live on earth, often despised and unnoticed but dwelling under the protection of heaven; they eagerly desire the Gospel.

That there were shepherds means that no one is to hear the Gospel for himself alone, but every one is to tell it to others who are not acquainted with it. For he who believes for himself has enough and should endeavor to bring others to such faith and knowledge, so that one may be a shepherd of the other, to wait upon and lead him into the pasture of the Gospel in this world, during the nighttime of this earthly life. At first the shepherds were sore afraid because of the angel; for human nature is shocked when it first hears in the Gospel that all our works are nothing and are condemned before God, for it does not easily give up its prejudices and presumptions.

Therefore let us beware of all teaching that does not set forth Christ. What more would you know?

What more do you need, if indeed you know Christ, as above set forth, if you walk by faith in God, and by love to your neighbor, doing to him as Christ has done to you. This is indeed the whole Scripture in its briefest form: that no more words or books are necessary, but only life and action.

Let everyone examine himself in the light of the Gospel and see how far he is from Christ, and what is the character of his faith and love. There are many who are enkindled with dreamy devotion, and when they hear of the poverty of Christ, they are almost angry with the citizens of Bethlehem. They denounce their blindness and ingratitude, and think, if they had been there, they would have shown the Lord and his mother a more kindly service, and would not have permitted them to be treated so miserably. But they do not look by their side to see how many of their fellow humans need their help, and which they ignore in their misery. Who is there upon earth that has no poor, miserable, sick, erring ones around him? Why does he not exercise his love to those? Why does he not do to them as Christ has done to him?

The Mystery

St. John Chrysostom

Suddenly a great company of the heavenly host appeared with the angel, praising God and saying, "Glory to God in the highest, and on earth peace to men on whom his favor rests."

I BEHOLD A NEW and wondrous mystery. My ears resound to the shepherds' song, piping no soft melody, but chanting full forth a heavenly hymn. The angels sing. The archangels blend their voice in harmony. The cherubim hymn their joyful praise. The seraphim exalt his glory. All join to praise this holy feast, beholding the Godhead here on earth, and man in heaven. He who is above, now for our redemption dwells here below; and he that was lowly is by divine mercy raised up.

Bethlehem this day resembles heaven; hearing from the stars the singing of angelic voices; and in place of the sun, enfolding within itself on every side, the Sun of Justice. And ask not how: for where God wills, the order of nature yields. For he willed, he had the power, he descended, he redeemed; all things move in obedience to God. This day he who is, is born; and he who is, becomes what he was not. For when he was God, he became man; yet not departing from the Godhead that is his. Nor yet by any loss of divinity became he man, nor through increase became he God from man; but being the Word he became flesh, his nature remaining unchanged.

The Father begot in the Spirit, and the Virgin brought forth without defilement. The Father begot without the limitations of flesh; so neither did the Virgin endure corruption in her childbearing, since she brought forth miraculously. Hence, since this heavenly birth cannot be described, neither does his coming amongst us in these days permit of too curious scrutiny. Though I know that a virgin this day gave birth, and I believe that God was begotten before all time, yet the manner of this birth I have learned to venerate in silence, and I accept that this is not to be probed too curiously with wordy speech. For with God we look not for the order of nature, but rest our faith in the power of his works.

It is indeed the way of nature that a woman in wedlock brings forth new life; when an unwed virgin, after she has born a child, is still a virgin, then nature here is surpassed. Of that which happens in accord with nature we may inquire; what transcends it we honor in silence; not as something to be avoided, passed over, but as that which we venerate in silence, as something sublime, beyond all telling.

What shall I say to you; what shall I tell you? I behold a mother who has brought forth new life; I see a child come to this light by birth. The manner of his conception I cannot comprehend. Nature here is overcome, the boundaries of the established order set aside, where God so wills. For not according to nature has this thing come to pass. Nature here has rested, while the will of God labored. O, ineffable grace! The only begotten One, who is before all ages, who cannot be touched or be perceived, who is simple, without body, has now put on my body, which is visible and liable to corruption. For what reason? That coming amongst us he may teach us, and teaching, lead us by the hand to the things that we mortals cannot see. For since we believe that the eyes are more trustworthy than the ears, we doubt that which they do not see, and so he has deigned to show himself in bodily presence, that he may remove all doubt.

And he was born from a virgin, who knew not his purpose; neither had she labored with him to bring it to pass, nor contributed to that which he had done, but was the simple instrument of his hidden power. That alone she knew which she had learned by her question to Gabriel: "How shall this be done, because I know not a man?" Then said he: "The Holy Spirit shall come upon thee, and the power of the Most High shall overshadow thee."

And in what manner was the Almighty with her, who came forth from her? He was as the craftsman, who coming on some suitable material, fashions to himself a beautiful vessel; so Christ, finding the holy body and soul of the Virgin, builds for himself a living temple, and as he had willed, formed there a man from the Virgin; and, putting him on, this day came forth; unashamed of the lowliness of our nature. For it was to him no lowering to put on what he himself had made. Let that handiwork be forever glorified, which became the cloak of its own creator. For as in the first creation of flesh, man could not be made before the clay had come into his hand, so neither could this corruptible body be glorified, until it had first become the garment of its maker.

What shall I say! And how shall I describe this birth to you? For this wonder fills me with astonishment. The Ancient of Days has become an infant. He who sits upon the sublime and heavenly throne now lies in a manger. And he who cannot be touched, who is without complexity, incorporeal, now lies subject to human hands. He who has broken the bonds of sinners is now bound by an infant's bands. But he has decreed that ignominy shall become honor, infamy be clothed with glory, and abject humiliation the measure of his goodness. For this he assumed my body, that I may become capable of his word; taking my flesh, he gives me his spirit; and so he bestowing and I receiving, he prepares for me the treasure of life. He takes my flesh to sanctify me; he gives me his Spirit, that he may save me.

Truly wondrous is the whole chronicle of the nativity. For this day the ancient slavery is ended, the devil confounded, the demons take to flight, the power of death is broken. For this day paradise is unlocked, the curse is taken away, sin is removed, error driven out, truth has been brought back, the speech of kindliness diffused and spread on every side – a heavenly way of life has been implanted on the earth, angels communicate with men without fear, and we now hold speech with angels.

Why is this? Because God is now on earth, and man in heaven; on every side all things commingle. He has come on earth, while being fully in heaven; and while complete in heaven, he is without diminution on earth. Though he was God, he became man, not denying himself to be God. Though being the unchanging Word, he became flesh that he might dwell amongst us.

What shall I say? What shall I utter? "Behold an infant wrapped in swaddling clothes and lying in a manger." Mary is present, who is both virgin and mother. Joseph is present, who is called father. He is called husband, she is called wife. The names indeed are lawful, but there is no other bond. We speak here of words, not of "realities."

To Him, then, who out of confusion has wrought a clear path; to Christ, to the Father, and to the Holy Spirit, we offer all praise, now and forever. Amen.

Ox and Ass

Giovanni Papini

JESUS WAS BORN IN A STABLE, a real stable, not
the bright, airy portico which Christian painters
have created for the Son of David, as if ashamed that
their God should have lain down in poverty and dirt.
And not the modern Christmas Eve "holy stable"
either, made of plaster of Paris, with little candy-like
statuettes, the holy stable, clean and prettily painted,
with a neat, tidy manger, an ecstatic ass, a contrite
ox, and angels fluttering their wreaths on the roof –
this is not the stable where Jesus was born.

A real stable is the house, the prison of the animals who work for man. The poor, old stable of
Christ's old, poor country is only four rough walls, a
dirty pavement, a roof of beams and slate. It is dark,

reeking. The only clean thing in it is the manger where the owner piles the hay and fodder.

Fresh in the clear morning, waving in the wind, sunny, lush, sweet-scented, the spring meadow was mown. The green grass, the long, slim blades, were cut down by the scythe; and with the grass the beautiful flowers in full bloom – white, red, yellow, blue. They withered and dried and took on the one dull color of hay. Oxen dragged back to the barn the dead plunder of May and June. And now that grass has become dry hay and those flowers, still smelling sweet, are there in the manger to feed the slaves of man. The animals take it slowly with their great black lips, and later the flowering fields, changed into moist dung, return to light on the litter which serves as bedding.

This is the real stable where Jesus was born. The filthiest place in the world was the first room of the only pure man ever born of woman. The Son of Man, who was to be devoured by wild beasts calling themselves men, had as his first cradle the manger where the animals chewed the cud of the miraculous flowers of spring.

It was not by chance that Christ was born in a stable. What is the world but an immense stable where men produce filth and wallow in it? Do they not daily change the most beautiful, the purest, the most divine things into excrement? Then, stretching themselves at full length on the piles of manure, they say they are "enjoying life." Upon this earthly pigsty, where no decorations or perfumes can hide the odor of filth, Jesus appeared one night, born of a stainless Virgin armed only with innocence...

First to worship Jesus were animals, not men. Among men he sought out the simple-hearted: among the simple-hearted he sought out children. Simpler than children, and milder, the beasts of burden welcomed him.

Though humble, though servants of beings weaker and fiercer than they, the ass and the ox had seen multitudes kneeling before them. Christ's own people, the people of Jehovah, the chosen people whom Jehovah had freed from Egyptian slavery, when their leader left them alone in the desert to go up and talk with the Eternal, did they not force Aaron to make them a golden calf to worship? In

Greece the ass was sacred to Ares, to Dionysius, to Hyperborean Apollo. Balaam's ass, wiser than the prophet, saved him by speaking. Oxus, King of Persia, put an ass in the temple of Ptha, and had it worshiped. And Augustus, Christ's temporal sovereign, had set up in the temple the brazen statue of an ass, to commemorate the good omen of his meeting on the eve of Actium an ass named "the Victorious."

Up to that time the kings of the earth and the populace craving material things had bowed before oxen and asses. But Jesus did not come into the world to reign over the earth, nor to love material things. He was to bring to an end the bowing down before beasts, the weakness of Aaron, the superstition of Augustus. The beasts of Jerusalem will murder him, but in the meantime the beasts of Bethlehem warm him with their breath. In later years, when Jesus went up to the city of death for the Feast of the Passover, he was mounted on an ass. But he was a greater prophet than Balaam, coming not to save the Jews alone but all men: and he did not turn back from his path, no, not though all the mules of Jerusalem brayed against him.

The Christmas Gospel

Dorothee Soelle

When the angels had left them and gone into heaven, the shepherds said to one another, "Let us go now to Bethlehem and see this thing that has taken place, which the Lord has made known to us." So they went with haste and found Mary and Joseph, and the child lying in the manger. When they saw this, they made known what had been told them about this child; and all who heard it were amazed at what the shepherds told them. But Mary treasured all these words and pondered them in her heart. The shepherds returned, glorifying God for all they had heard and seen, as it had been told them.

LUKE 2:15–20

FOR MANY YEARS I WAS so disgusted by the commercialization that Christmas has endured, so sickened by the terror of consumption, the pressures of buying, giving, and eating, that I did not want even to think of Luke 2. The violent context in which we live had blocked the light of the text, which seemed to me hopelessly instrumentalized for lies. The baby in the manger was embarrassing, like rich almond candy.

The escape of the yuppies – to run away and have a few beautiful days without fuss – was not available to me for family reasons. Instead we attempted to work in the context, to locate the stable in a homeless shelter in Cologner-Mulheim and to find the shepherds again among marginalized youths and vagabonds. They told the story in their way and thereby contributed to our liberation. The text itself remained a piece from the museum. That changed at the end of the seventies, when I learned something historically that had not occurred to me in study and exegesis.

I understood rather late what the tyranny of the *imperium romanum* really meant for the people in the subjugated provinces. Up to this moment I held unsuspectingly to my humanist illusions about the *pax romana*. I regarded it as a kind of constitutional state with a cosmopolitan trading system and grandiose architecture. I had learned to read history only with the eyes of the victor. That the *pax Christi* was intended precisely for those who could expect nothing from the *pax romana* gave me a new key to the Christmas narrative and to the whole New Testament. How and under what conditions had people lived then in Galilee? Why had I never noticed the number of sick who appear in the Gospels? Who or what made them sick? Political oppression, legal degradation, economic plunder, and religious neutrality in the scope of the *religio licita* ("permitted religion") were realities that the writer Luke kept in view in his story, which is so sublime and yet so focused on the center of all conceivable power. At last I saw the *imperium* from the perspective of those dominated by it. I recognized torturers and informers behind the coercive measure, "All went…to be registered" (v. 3). Finally I comprehended the peace of the angels "on earth" and not only in the souls of individual people. I understood for the first time the propaganda terms of the Roman writers who spoke of *pax* and *jus* when they really meant grain prices and militarization of the earth known at that time. (All this can be confirmed by research today.)

Of course, my rereading was politically colored. I too was surrounded by propaganda (freedom and democracy). While I heard the boot of the empire crush everything in its way in the narrative from Bethlehem to Golgotha, I saw the carpet bombings in the poor districts of San Salvador right behind the glittering displays on Fifth Avenue in New York… In Paul these causes of misery are called the reign of sin. Without understanding this *imperium* in its economic and ecological power of death, we also cannot see the light of Christmas shine. Living in the pretended social market economy, we do not even seem to need this light!

Whoever wants to proclaim something about this light has to free the stifled longing of people. An interpretation of the Bible that takes seriously concrete, everyday human cares and does not make light of the dying of children from hunger and neglect is helpful in this regard. By showing up the incomparable power of violence in our world today, it deepens our yearning for true peace.

Our text refers to the praxis of transmission and proclamation. The frightened shepherds become God's messengers. They organize, make haste, find others, and speak with them. Do we not all want to become shepherds and catch sight of the angel? I think so. Without the perspective of the poor, we see nothing, not even an angel. When we approach the poor, our values and goals change. The child appears in many other children. Mary also seeks sanctuary among us. Because the angels sing, the shepherds rise, leave their fears behind, and set out for Bethlehem, wherever it is situated these days.

The Grand Miracle

C. S. *Lewis*

SUPPOSING YOU HAD before you a manuscript of some great work, either a symphony or a novel. There then comes to you a person, saying, "Here is a new bit of the manuscript that I found; it is the central passage of that symphony, or the central chapter of that novel. The text is incomplete without it. I have got the missing passage which is really the center of the whole work." The only thing you could do would be to put this new piece of the manuscript in that central position, and then see how it reflected on the whole of the rest of the work. If it constantly brought out new meanings from the whole of the rest of the work, if it made you notice things in the rest of the work which you had not noticed before, then I think you would decide that it was authentic. On the other hand, if it failed to do that, then, however attractive it was in itself, you would reject it.

Now, what is the missing chapter in this case, the chapter which Christians are offering? The story of the Incarnation – the story of a descent and resurrection. When I say "resurrection" here, I am not referring simply to the first few hours, or the first few weeks of the Resurrection. I am talking of this whole, huge pattern of descent, down, down, and then up again. What we ordinarily call the Resurrection being just, so to speak, the point at which it turns. Think what that descent is. The coming down, not only into humanity, but into those nine months which precede human birth, in which they tell us we all recapitulate strange pre-human, sub-human forms of life, and going lower still into being a corpse, a thing which, if this ascending movement had not begun, would presently have passed out of the organic altogether, and have gone back into the inorganic, as all corpses do. One has a picture of someone going right down and dredging the sea-bottom. One has a picture of a strong man trying to lift a very big, complicated burden. He stoops down and gets himself right under it so that he himself disappears; and then he straightens his back and moves off with the whole thing swaying on his shoulders. Or else one has the picture of a diver, stripping off garment after garment, making himself naked, then flashing for a moment in the air, and then down through the green and warm and sunlit water into the pitch black, cold, freezing water, down into the mud and slime, then up again, his lungs almost bursting, back again to the green and warm and sunlit water, and then at last out into the sunshine, holding in his hand the dripping thing he went down to get. This thing is human nature; but associated with it, all nature, the new universe. That indeed is a point I cannot go into here, because it would take a whole sermon – this connection between human nature and nature in general. It sounds startling, but I believe it can be fully justified.

Now as soon as you have thought of this, this pattern of the huge dive down to the bottom, into the depths of the universe and coming up again into the light, everyone will see at once how that is imitated and echoed by the principles of the natural world; the descent of the seed into the soil, and its rising again in the plants. There are also all sorts of things in our own spiritual life, where a thing has to be killed, and broken, in order that it may then become bright and strong and splendid. The analogy is obvious…

In the Incarnation we get, of course, the idea of vicariousness of one person profiting by the earning of another person. In its highest form that is the very center of Christianity. And we also find this same vicariousness to be a characteristic, or, as the musician would put it, a *leit-motif* of nature. It is a law of the natural universe that no being can exist on its own resources. Everyone, everything, is hopelessly indebted to everyone and everything else. In the universe, as we now see it, this is the source of many of the greatest horrors: all the horrors of carnivorousness, and the worse horrors of the parasites, those horrible animals that live under the skin of other animals, and so on. And yet, suddenly seeing it in the light of the Christian story, one realizes that vicariousness is not in itself bad; that all these animals and insects and horrors are merely that principle of vicariousness twisted in one way. For when you think it out, nearly everything good in nature also comes from vicariousness. After all, the child, both before and after birth, lives on its mother, just as the parasite lives on its host, the one being a horror, the other being the source of almost every natural goodness in the world. It all depends upon what you do with this principle. What is implied by the Incarnation just fits in exactly with what I have seen in nature, and (this is the important point) each time it gives it a new twist. If I accept this supposed missing chapter, the Incarnation, I find it begins to illuminate the whole of the rest of the manuscript. It lights up nature's pattern…

That is why I think this Grand Miracle is the missing chapter in this novel, the chapter on which the whole plot turns; that is why I believe that God really has dived down into the bottom of creation, and has come up bringing the whole redeemed nature on His shoulders. The miracles that have already happened are, of course, as Scripture so often says, the first fruits of that cosmic summer which is presently coming on. Christ has risen, and so we shall rise. St. Peter for a few seconds walks on the water; and the day will come when there will be a remade universe, infinitely obedient to the will of glorified and obedient men, when we can do all things, when we shall be those gods that we are described as being in Scripture. To be sure, it feels wintry enough still: but often in the very early spring it feels like that. Two thousand years are only a day or two by this scale. A man really ought to say, "The Resurrection happened two thousand years ago" in the same spirit in which he says, "I saw a crocus yesterday." Because we know what is coming behind the crocus. The spring comes slowly down this way; but the great thing is that the corner has been turned. There is, of course, this difference that in the natural spring the crocus cannot choose whether it will respond or not. We can. We have the power either of withstanding the spring, and sinking back into the cosmic winter, or of going on into those "high mid-summer pomps" in which our Leader, the Son of Man, already dwells, and to which He is calling us. It remains with us to follow or not, to die in this winter, or to go on into that spring and that summer.

Christ's History, and Ours

Gustavo Gutiérrez

THE GOSPEL OF LUKE tells us that "In those days a decree went out from Caesar Augustus that the whole world should be enrolled. This was the first enrollment, when Quirinius was governor of Syria" (2:1–2). The Gospel of Matthew adds that Jesus was born "in Bethlehem of Judea, in the days of King Herod" (2:1).

These simple texts convey a profound message: Jesus was born in a particular place at a particular time. He was born under Emperor Octavius, who had himself named Augustus when he reached the pinnacle of power; when Quirinius was governor of Syria; during the reign of Herod, who was traitor to his people and had sold out to the occupying power. It was during this time that Jesus was born, a man of no importance in the eyes of the cynical and arrogant authorities as well as in the eyes of those who disguised cowardice as peace and political realism.

He was born in Bethlehem, "one of the little clans of Judah" (Mi. 5:2), where at his birth he was surrounded by shepherds and their flocks. His parents had come to a stable after vainly knocking at numerous doors in the town, as the Gospels tell us; we are reminded of the popular Mexican custom of *las posadas*. There, on the fringe of society, the Word became history, contingency, solidarity, and weakness; but we can say, too, that by this becoming, history itself, our history, became Word.

It is often said at Christmas that Jesus is born into every family and every heart. But these "births" must not make us forget the primordial, massive fact that Jesus was born of Mary among a people that at the time were dominated by the greatest empire of the age. If we forget that fact, the birth of Jesus becomes an abstraction, a symbol, a cipher. Apart from its historical coordinates the event loses its meaning. To

the eyes of Christians the incarnation is the irruption of God into human history: an incarnation into
littleness and service in the midst of overbearing
power exercised by the mighty of this world; an irruption that smells of the stable.

The Son of God was born into a little people, a
nation of little importance by comparison with the
great powers of the time. Furthermore, he took flesh
among the poor in a marginal area – namely, Galilee; he lived with the poor and emerged from among
them to inaugurate a kingdom of love and justice.
That is why many have trouble recognizing him. The
God who became flesh in Jesus is the hidden God of
whom the prophets speak to us. Jesus shows himself
to be such precisely in the measure that he is present
via those who are the absent, anonymous people of
history – those who are not the controllers of history,
namely, the mighty, the socially acceptable, "the wise
and the learned" (Mt. 11:25).

Christian faith is a historical faith. God is revealed in Jesus Christ and, through him, in human
history and in the least important and poorest sector
of those who make it up. Only with this as a starting
point is it possible to believe in God. Believers can-

not go aside into a kind of dead-end corner of history and watch it go by. It is in the concrete setting and circumstances of our lives that we must learn to believe: under oppression and repression but also amid the struggles and hopes that are alive in present-day Latin America; under dictatorships that sow death among the poor, and under the "democracies" that often deal unjustly with their needs and dreams.

The Lord is not intimidated by the darkness or by the rejection of his own. His light is stronger than all the shadows. If we are to dwell in the tent the Son has pitched in our midst, we must enter into our own history here and now, and nourish our hope on the will to life that the poor of our continent are demonstrating. If we do so, we shall experience in our flesh the encounter with the Word who proclaims the kingdom of life.

The Visited Planet

Philip Yancey

SORTING THROUGH THE STACK of cards that arrived at our house last Christmas, I note that all
kinds of symbols have edged their way into the celebration. Overwhelmingly, the landscape scenes
render New England towns buried in snow, usually
with the added touch of a horse-drawn sleigh. On
other cards, animals frolic: not only reindeer but also
chipmunks, raccoons, cardinals and cute gray mice.
One card shows an African lion reclining with a
foreleg draped affectionately around a lamb.

Angels have made a huge comeback in recent
years, and Hallmark and American Greetings now
feature them prominently, though as demure, cud-

dly-looking creatures, not the type who would ever need to announce "Fear not!" The explicitly religious cards (a distinct minority) focus on the holy family, and you can tell at a glance these folk are different. They seem unruffled and serene. Bright gold halos, like crowns from another world, hover just above their heads.

Inside, the cards stress sunny words like love, goodwill, cheer, happiness, and warmth. It is a fine thing, I suppose, that we honor a sacred holiday with such homey sentiments. And yet when I turn to the gospel accounts of the first Christmas, I hear a very different tone, and sense mainly disruption at work...

Even those who accept the supernatural version of events concede that big trouble will follow: an old uncle prays for "salvation from our enemies and from the hand of all who hate us"; Simeon darkly warns the virgin that "a sword will pierce your own soul too"; Mary's hymn of thanksgiving mentions rulers overthrown and proud men scattered.

In contrast to what the cards would have us believe, Christmas did not sentimentally simplify life on planet earth. Perhaps this is what I sense when

Christmas rolls around and I turn from the cheeriness of the cards to the starkness of the Gospels.

Christmas art depicts Jesus' family as icons stamped in gold foil, with a calm Mary receiving the tidings of the Annunciation as a kind of benediction. But that is not at all how Luke tells the story. Mary was "greatly troubled" and "afraid" at the angel's appearance, and when the angel pronounced the sublime words about the Son of the Most High whose kingdom will never end, Mary had something far more mundane on her mind: *But I am a virgin!*

Once, a young unmarried lawyer bravely stood before my church in Chicago and told of a sin we already knew about: we had seen her hyperactive son running up and down the aisles every Sunday. Cynthia had taken the lonely road of bearing an illegitimate child and caring for him after his father decided to skip town. Cynthia's sin was no worse than many others, and yet, as she told us, it had such conspicuous consequences. She could not hide the result of that single act of passion, sticking out as it did from her abdomen for months until a child emerged to change every hour of every day of the rest of her life. No wonder the Jewish teenager Mary felt greatly troubled: she faced the same prospects even without the act of passion.

In the modern United States, where each year a million teenage girls get pregnant out of wedlock, Mary's predicament has undoubtedly lost some of its force, but in a closely knit Jewish community in the first century, the news an angel brought could not have been entirely welcome. The law regarded a betrothed woman who became pregnant as an adulteress, subject to death by stoning.

Matthew tells of Joseph magnanimously agreeing to divorce Mary in private rather than press charges, until an angel shows up to correct his perception of betrayal. Luke tells of a tremulous Mary hurrying off to the one person who could possibly understand what she was going through: her relative Elizabeth, who miraculously got pregnant in old age after another angelic annunciation. Elizabeth believes Mary and shares her joy, and yet the scene poignantly highlights the contrast between the two women: the whole countryside is talking about Elizabeth's healed womb even as Mary must hide the shame of her own miracle.

In a few months, the birth of John the Baptist took place amid great fanfare, complete with midwives, doting relatives, and the traditional village chorus celebrating the birth of a Jewish male. Six months later, Jesus was born far from home, with no midwife, extended family, or village chorus present. A male head of household would have sufficed for the Roman census; did Joseph drag his pregnant wife along to Bethlehem in order to spare her the ignominy of childbirth in her home village?...

Nine months of awkward explanations, the lingering scent of scandal – it seems that God arranged the most humiliating circumstances possible for his entrance, as if to avoid any charge of favoritism. I am impressed that when the Son of God became a human being he played by the rules, harsh rules: small towns do not treat kindly young boys who grow up with questionable paternity.

Malcolm Muggeridge observed that in our day, with family-planning clinics offering convenient ways to correct "mistakes" that might disgrace a family name, "It is, in point of fact, extremely improbable, under existing conditions, that Jesus would have been permitted to be born at all. Mary's pregnancy, in poor circumstances, and with the father unknown, would have been an obvious case for an abortion; and her talk of having conceived as a result of the intervention of the Holy Ghost would have pointed to the need for psychiatric treatment, and made the case for terminating her pregnancy even stronger. Thus our generation, needing a Savior more, perhaps, than any that has ever existed, would be too 'humane' to allow one to be born."

The virgin Mary, though, whose parenthood was unplanned, had a different response. She heard the angel out, pondered the repercussions, and replied, "I am the Lord's servant. May it be to me as you have said." Often a work of God comes with two edges, great joy and great pain, and in that matter-of-fact response Mary embraced both. She was the first person to accept Jesus on his own terms, regardless of the personal cost.

When the Jesuit missionary Matteo Ricci went to China in the sixteenth century, he brought along samples of religious art to illustrate the Christian story for people who had never heard it. The Chinese readily adopted portraits of the Virgin Mary holding her child, but when he produced paintings of the crucifixion and tried to explain that the God-child had grown up only to be executed, the audience reacted with revulsion and horror. They much preferred the Virgin and insisted on worshiping her rather than the crucified God.

As I thumb once more through my stack of Christmas cards, I realize that we in Christian countries do much the same thing. We observe a mellow, domesticated holiday purged of any hint of scandal. Above all, we purge from it any reminder of how the story that began in Bethlehem turned out at Calvary.

In the birth stories of Luke and Matthew, only one person seems to grasp the mysterious nature of what God has set in motion: the old man Simeon, who recognized the baby as the Messiah, instinctively understood that conflict would surely follow. "This child is destined to cause the falling and rising of many in Israel, and to be a sign that will be spoken against..." he said, and then made the prediction that a sword would pierce Mary's own soul. Somehow Simeon sensed that though on the surface little had changed – the autocrat Herod still ruled, Roman troops were still stringing up patriots, Jerusalem still overflowed with beggars – underneath, everything had changed. A new force had arrived to undermine the world's powers…

The earliest events in Jesus' life, though, give a menacing preview of the unlikely struggle now under way. Herod, King of the Jews, enforced Roman rule at the local level, and in an irony of history we know Herod's name mainly because of the massacre of the innocents. I have never seen a Christmas card depicting that state-sponsored act of terror, but it too was a part of Christ's coming. Although secular history does not refer to the atrocity, no one acquainted with the life of Herod doubts him capable. He killed two brothers-in-law, his own wife Mariamne, and two of his own sons. Five days before his death he ordered the arrest of many citizens and decreed that they be executed on the day of his death, in order to guarantee a proper atmosphere of mourning in the country. For such a despot, a minor extermination procedure in Bethlehem posed no problem.

Scarcely a day passed, in fact, without an execution under Herod's regime. The political climate at the time of Jesus' birth resembled that of Russia in the 1930s under Stalin. Citizens could not gather in public meetings. Spies were everywhere. In Herod's mind, the command to slaughter Bethlehem's infants was probably an act of utmost rationality, a rearguard action to preserve the stability of his kingdom against a rumored invasion from another...

And so Jesus the Christ entered the world amid strife and terror, and spent his infancy hidden in Egypt as a refugee. Matthew notes that local politics even determined where Jesus would grow up. When Herod the Great died, an angel reported to Joseph it was safe for him to return to Israel, but not to the region where Herod's son Archelaus had taken command. Joseph moved his family instead to Nazareth in the north, where they lived under the domain of another of Herod's sons, Antipas, the one Jesus would call "that fox," and also the one who would have John the Baptist beheaded.

A few years later the Romans took over direct command of the southern province that encompassed Jerusalem, and the cruelest and most notorious of these governors was a man named Pontius Pilate. Well-connected, Pilate had married the granddaughter of Augustus Caesar. According to Luke, Herod Antipas and the Roman governor Pilate regarded each other as enemies until the day fate brought them together to determine the destiny of Jesus. On that day they collaborated, hoping to succeed where Herod the Great had failed; by disposing of the strange pretender and thus preserving the kingdom.

From beginning to end, the conflict between Rome and Jesus appeared to be entirely one-sided. The execution of Jesus would put an apparent end to any threat, or so it was assumed at the time. Tyranny would win again. It occurred to no one that his stubborn followers just might outlast the Roman empire...

As I read the birth stories about Jesus I cannot help but conclude that though the world may be tilted toward the rich and powerful, God is tilted toward the underdog. "He has brought down rulers from their thrones but lifted up the humble. He has filled the hungry with good things but sent the rich away empty," said Mary in her Magnificat...

I wonder what Mary thought about her militant hymn during her harrowing years in Egypt. For a Jew, Egypt evoked bright memories of a powerful God who had flattened a pharaoh's army and brought liberation; now Mary fled there, desperate, a stranger in a strange land hiding from her own government. Could her baby, hunted, helpless, on the run, possibly fulfill the lavish hopes of his people?

Even the family's mother-tongue summoned up memories of their underdog status: Jesus spoke Aramaic, a trade language closely related to Arabic, a stinging reminder of the Jews' subjection to foreign empires.

Some foreign astrologers (probably from the region that is now Iraq) had dropped by to visit Jesus, but these men were considered "unclean" by Jews of the day. Naturally, like all dignitaries they had checked first with the ruling king in Jerusalem, who knew nothing about a baby in Bethlehem. After they saw the child and realized who he was, these visitors engaged in an act of civil disobedience: they deceived Herod and went home another way, to protect the child. They had chosen Jesus' side against the powerful.

Growing up, Jesus' sensibilities were affected most deeply by the poor, the powerless, the oppressed – in short, the underdogs. Today theologians debate the aptness of the phrase "God's preferential option for the poor" as a way of describing God's concern for the underdog. Since God arranged the circumstances in which to be born on planet earth – without power or wealth, without rights, without justice – his preferential options speak for themselves...

There is one more view of Christmas I have never seen on a Christmas card, probably because no artist, not even William Blake, could do it justice. Revelation 12 pulls back the curtain to give us a glimpse of Christmas as it must have looked from somewhere far beyond Andromeda: Christmas from the angels' viewpoint.

The account differs radically from the birth stories in the Gospels. Revelation does not mention shepherds and an infanticidal king; rather, it pictures a dragon leading a ferocious struggle in heaven. A woman clothed with the sun and wearing a crown of twelve stars cries out in pain as she is about to give birth. Suddenly the enormous red dragon enters the picture, his tail sweeping a third of the stars out of the sky and flinging them to the earth. He crouches hungrily before the woman, anxious to devour her child the moment it is born. At the last second the infant is snatched away to safety, the woman flees into the desert, and all-out cosmic war begins.

Revelation is a strange book by any measure, and readers must understand its style to make sense of this extraordinary spectacle. In daily life two parallel histories occur simultaneously, one on earth and one in heaven. Revelation, however, views them together, allowing a quick look behind the scenes. On earth a baby was born, a king caught wind of it, a chase ensued. In heaven the Great Invasion had begun, a daring raid by the ruler of the forces of good into the universe's seat of evil.

John Milton expressed this point of view majestically in *Paradise Lost* and *Paradise Regained*, poems which make heaven and hell the central focus and earth a mere battleground for their clashes. The modern author J. B. Phillips also attempted such a point of view, on a much less epic scale, and last Christmas I turned to Phillips' fantasy to try to escape my earthbound viewpoint.

In Phillips' version, a senior angel is showing a very young angel around the splendors of the universe. They view whirling galaxies and blazing suns, and then flit across the infinite distances of space until at last they enter one particular galaxy of 500 billion stars:

As the two of them drew near to the star which we call our sun and to its circling planets, the senior angel pointed to a small and rather insignificant sphere turning very slowly on its axis. It looked as dull as a dirty tennis-ball to the little angel, whose mind was filled with the size and glory of what he had seen.

"I want you to watch that one particularly," said the senior angel, pointing with his finger.

"Well, it looks very small and rather dirty to me," said the little angel. "What's special about that one?"

When I read Phillips' fantasy, I thought of the pictures beamed back to earth from the Apollo astronauts, who described our planet as "whole and round and beautiful and small," a blue-green-and-tan globe suspended in space. Jim Lovell, reflecting on the scene later, said, "It was just another body, really, about four times bigger than the moon. But it held all the hope and all the life and all the things that the crew of the Apollo 8 knew and loved. It was the most beautiful thing there was to see in all the heavens." That was the viewpoint of a human being.

To the little angel, though, earth did not seem so impressive. He listened in stunned disbelief as the senior angel told him that this planet, small and insignificant and not overly clean, was the renowned Visited Planet:

> "Do you mean that our great and glorious Prince... went down in Person to this fifth-rate little ball? Why should He do a thing like that?"...
>
> The little angel's face wrinkled in disgust. "Do you mean to tell me," he said, "that He stooped so low as to become one of those creeping, crawling creatures of that floating ball?"
>
> "I do, and I don't think He would like you to call them 'creeping, crawling creatures' in that tone of voice. For, strange as it may seem to us, He loves them. He went down to visit them to lift them up to become like Him."
>
> The little angel looked blank. Such a thought was almost beyond his comprehension.

It is almost beyond my comprehension too, and yet I accept that this notion is the key to understanding Christmas and is, in fact, the touchstone of my faith. As a Christian I believe that we live in parallel worlds. One world consists of hills and lakes and barns and politicians and shepherds watching their flocks by night. The other consists of angels and sinister forces and somewhere out there places called heaven and hell. One night in the cold, in the dark, among the wrinkled hills of Bethlehem, those two worlds came together at a dramatic point of intersection. God, who knows no before or after, entered time and space. God, who knows no boundaries, took on the shocking confines of a baby's skin, the ominous restraints of mortality.

"He is the image of the invisible God, the first-born over all creation," an apostle would later write; "He is before all things, and in him all things hold together." But the few eyewitnesses on Christmas night saw none of that. They saw an infant struggling to work never-before-used lungs.

Could it be true, this Bethlehem story of a Creator descending to be born on one small planet? If so, it is a story like no other. Never again need we wonder whether what happens on this dirty little tennis ball of a planet matters to the rest of the universe. Little wonder a choir of angels broke out in spontaneous song, disturbing not only a few shepherds but the entire universe.

The Time of No Room

Thomas Merton

He who has come to men
dwells where we cannot tell
nor sight reveal him,
until the hour has struck
when the small heart does break
with hunger for him;

those who do merit least,
those whom no tongue does praise
the first to know him,
and on the face of the earth
the poorest village street
blossoming for him.

JANE TYSON CLEMENT

SO THERE WAS NO ROOM at the inn? True! But that is simply mentioned in passing, in a matter-of-fact sort of way, as the Evangelist points to what he really means us to see – the picture of pure peace, pure joy: "She wrapped her firstborn Son in swaddling clothes and laid him in a manger" (Luke 2:7). By now we know it well, and yet we might still be questioning it – except that a reason was given for an act that might otherwise have seemed strange: "There was no room for them at the inn." Well, then, they obviously found some other place!

But when we read the Gospels and come to know them thoroughly, we realize there are other reasons why it was necessary that there be no room at the inn, and why there had to be some other place. In fact, the inn was the last place in the world for the birth of the Lord.

The Evangelists, preparing us for the announcement of the birth of the Lord, remind us that the fullness of time has come. Now is the time of final decision, the time of mercy, "the acceptable time," the time of settlement, the time of the end. It is the time of repentance, the time for the fulfillment of all promises, for the Promised One has come. But with the coming of the end, a great bustle and business begins to shake the nations of the world. The time of the end is the time of massed armies, "wars and rumors of wars," of huge crowds moving this way and that, of men "withering away for fear," of flaming cities and sinking fleets, of smoking lands laid waste, of technicians planning grandiose acts of destruction. The time of the end is the time of the Crowd: and the eschatological message is spoken in a world where, precisely because of the vast indefinite roar of armies on the move and the restlessness of turbulent mobs, the message can be heard only with difficulty. Yet it is heard by those who are aware that the display of power, *hubris* (power) and destruction is part of the *kerygma* (message). That which is to be judged announces itself, introduces itself by its sinister and arrogant claim to absolute power. Thus it is identified, and those who decide in favor of this claim are numbered, marked with the sign of power, aligned with power, and destroyed with it.

Why then was the inn crowded? Because of the census, the eschatological massing of the *"whole world"* in centers of registration, to be numbered, to be identified with the structure of imperial power.

The purpose of the census: to discover those who were to be taxed. To find out those who were eligible for service in the armies of the empire.

The Bible had not been friendly to a census in the days when God was ruler of Israel (2 Samuel 24). The numbering of the people of God by an alien emperor and their full consent to it was itself an eschatological sign, preparing those who could understand it to meet judgment with repentance. After all, in the Apocalyptic literature of the Bible, this "summoning together" or convocation of the powers of the earth to do battle is the great sign of "the end."

It was therefore impossible that the Word should lose himself by being born into shapeless and passive mass. He had indeed emptied himself, taken the form of God's servant, man. But he did not empty himself to the point of becoming mass man, faceless man. It was therefore right that there should be no room for him in a crowd that had been called together as an eschatological sign. His being born outside that crowd is even more of a sign. That there is no room for him is a sign of the end.

Nor are the tidings of great joy announced in the crowded inn. In the massed crowd there are always new tidings of joy and disaster. Where each new announcement is the greatest of announcements, where every day's disaster is beyond compare, every day's danger demands the ultimate sacrifice, all news and all judgment is reduced to zero. News becomes merely a new noise in the mind, briefly replacing the noise that went before it and yielding to the noise that comes after it, so that eventually everything blends into the same monotonous and meaningless rumor. News? There is so much news that there is no room left for the true tidings, the "Good News," *the Great Joy.*

Hence the Great Joy is announced, after all, in silence, loneliness and darkness, to shepherds "living in the fields" or "living in the countryside" and apparently unmoved by the rumors or massed crowds. These are the remnant of the desert-dwellers, the nomads, the true Israel.

Even though "the whole world" is ordered to be inscribed, they do not seem to be affected. Doubtless they have registered, as Joseph and Mary will register, but they remain outside the agitation, and untouched by the vast movement, the massing of hundreds and thousands of people everywhere in the towns and cities.

They are therefore quite otherwise signed. They are designated, surrounded by a great light, they receive the message of the Great Joy, and they believe it with joy. They see the *Shekinah* over them, recognize themselves for what they are. They are the remnant, the people of no account, who are therefore chosen – the *anawim*. And they obey the light. Nor was anything else asked of them.

They go and see not a prophet, not a spirit, but the Flesh in which the glory of the Lord will be revealed and by which all men will be delivered from the power that is in the world, the power that seeks to destroy the world because the world is God's creation, the power that mimics creation, and in doing so, pillages and exhausts the resources of a bounteous God-given earth.

We live in the time of no room, which is the time of the end. The time when everyone is obsessed with lack of time, lack of space, with saving time, conquering space, projecting into time and space the anguish produced within them by the technological furies of size, volume, quantity, speed, number, price, power and acceleration.

The primordial blessing, "increase and multiply," has suddenly become a hemorrhage of terror. We are numbered in billions, and massed together, marshalled, numbered, marched here and there, taxed, drilled, armed, worked to the point of insensibility, dazed by information, drugged by entertainment, surfeited with everything, nauseated with the human race and with ourselves, nauseated with life.

As the end approaches, there is no room for nature. The cities crowd it off the face of the earth.

As the end approaches, there is no room for quiet. There is no room for solitude. There is no room for thought. There is no room for attention, for the awareness of our state.

In the time of the ultimate end, there is no room for man.

Those that lament the fact that there is no room for God must also be called to account for this. Have they perhaps added to the general crush by preaching a solid marble God that makes man alien to himself, a God that settles himself grimly like an implacable object in the inner heart of man and drives man out of himself in despair?

The time of the end is the time of demons who occupy the heart (pretending to be gods) so that man himself finds no room for himself in himself. He finds no space to rest in his own heart, not because it is full, but because it is void. If only he knew that the void itself, when hovered over by the Spirit, is an abyss of creativity...yet he cannot believe it. There is no room for belief.

In the time of the end there is no longer room for the desire to go on living. The time of the end is the time when men call upon the mountains to fall upon them, because they wish they did not exist.

Why? Because they are part of a proliferation of life that is not fully alive, it is programmed for death. A life that has not been chosen, and can hardly be accepted, has no more room for hope. Yet it must pretend to go on hoping. It is haunted by the demon of emptiness. And out of this unutterable void come the armies, the missiles, the weapons, the bombs, the concentration camps, the race riots, the racist murders, and all the other crimes of mass society.

Is this pessimism? Is this the unforgivable sin of admitting what everybody really feels? Is it pessimism to diagnose cancer as cancer? Or should one simply go on pretending that everything is getting better every day, because the time of the end is also – for some at any rate – the time of great prosperity? "The kings of the earth have joined in her idolatry, and the traders of the earth have grown rich from her excessive luxury" (Revelation 18:3).

Into this world, this demented inn, in which there is absolutely no room for him at all, Christ has come uninvited. But because he cannot be at home in it – because he is out of place in it, and yet must be in it – his place is with those others who do not belong, who are rejected because they are regarded as weak; and with those who are discredited, who are denied the status of persons, and are tortured, exterminated. With those for whom there is no room, Christ is present in this world. He is mysteriously present in those for whom there seems to be nothing but the world at its worst. For them, there is no escape even in imagination. They cannot identify with the power structure of a crowded humanity which seeks to project itself outward, anywhere, in a centrifugal flight into the void, to get *out there* where there is no God, no man, no name, no identity, no weight, no self, nothing but the bright, self-directed, perfectly obedient and infinitely expensive machine.

For those who are stubborn enough, devoted enough to power, there remains this last apocalyptic myth of machinery propagating its own kind in the eschatological wilderness of space – while on earth the bombs make room!

But the others: they remain imprisoned in other hopes, and in more pedestrian despairs, despairs and hopes which are held down to earth, down to street level, and to the pavement only: desire to be at least half-human, to taste a little human joy, to do a fairly decent job of productive work, to come home to the family…desires for which there is no room. It is in these that He hides himself, for whom there is no room.

The time of the end? All right: when?

That is not the question.

To say that it is the time of the end is to answer all the questions, for if it is the time of the end, and of great tribulation, then it is certainly and above all the time of the Great Joy. It is the time to "lift up your heads for your redemption is at hand." It is the time when the promise will be manifestly fulfilled, and no longer kept secret from anyone. It is the time for the joy that is given not as the world gives, and that no man can take away.

For the true eschatological banquet is not that of the birds on the bodies of the slain. It is the feast of the living, the wedding banquet of the Lamb. The true eschatological convocation is not the crowding of armies on the field of battle, but the summons of the Great Joy, the cry of deliverance: "Come out of her, my people, that you may not share in her sins and suffer from her plagues!" (Revelation 18:4). The cry of the time of the end was uttered also in the beginning by Lot in Sodom, to his sons-in-law: "Come, get out of this city, for the Lord will destroy it. But he seemed to them to be jesting" (Genesis 19:14).

To leave the city of death and imprisonment is surely not bad news except to those who have so identified themselves with their captivity that they can conceive no other reality and no other condition. In such a case, there is nothing but tribulation: for while to stay in captivity is tragic, to break away from it is unthinkable – and so more tragic still.

What is needed then is the grace and courage to see that "the Great Tribulation" and "the Great Joy" are really inseparable, and that the "Tribulation" becomes "Joy" when it is seen as the victory of life over death.

True, there is a sense in which there is no room for joy in this tribulation. To say there is "no room" for the Great Joy in the tribulation of "the end" is to say that the evangelical joy must not be confused with the joys proposed by the world in the time of the end – and, we must admit it, these are no longer convincing as joys. They become now stoic duties and sacrifices to be offered without question for ends that cannot be described just now, since there is too much smoke and the visibility is rather poor. In the last analysis, the "joy" proposed by the time of the end is simply the satisfaction and the relief of getting it all over with...

That is the demonic temptation of the "end." For eschatology is not *finis* and punishment, the winding up of accounts and the closing of books: it is the final beginning, the definitive birth into a new creation. It is not the last gasp of exhausted possibilities but the first taste of all that is beyond conceiving as actual.

But can we believe it? ("He seemed to them to be jesting!")

When the Time Was Fulfilled

Eberhard Arnold

Joseph went up to Bethlehem to register with Mary, who was pledged to be married to him and was expecting a child. While they were there, the time was fulfilled for the baby to be born, and she gave birth to her firstborn, a son.

LUKE 2:5–6

"WHEN THE TIME was fulfilled…" What a redeeming power there is in these words! We are concerned day in and day out with lesser or greater matters that are to serve God and his cause. We work sometimes until we are weary and yet we see so little fruit. Does everything remain as it was? Haven't we gone forward at all? Have we really been able to help a little somewhere, or have we merely affected the surface of things? Where is there a trace or glimpse of the goal we long for? What are all our efforts against the apparently indestructible powers of misery and evil?

It is well for us that at such hours the light is shining from the stable of Bethlehem and that we are able to sense what it means that the kingdom of God was born as a little child when the time was fulfilled.

Christmas did not come after a great mass of people had completed something good, or because of the successful result of any human effort. No, it came as a miracle, as the child that comes when his time is fulfilled, as a gift of the Father which he lays into those arms that are stretched out in longing. In this way did Christmas come; in this way it always comes anew, both to individuals and to the whole world.

You have perhaps waited for years to be freed from some need. For a long, long time you have looked out from the darkness in search of the light, and have had a difficult problem in life that you have not been able to solve in spite of great efforts. And then, when the time was fulfilled and God's hour had come, did not a solution, light, and deliverance come quite unexpectedly, perhaps quite differently than you thought? Hasn't this happened to you, just as the child comes at his own time, and no impatience or hurrying can compel it – but then it comes with its blessing and full of the wonder of God? Hasn't God's help come to us sometimes in this way?

And so it shall be with our yearning for the redemption of humanity and for a new shining forth of the world of God. When we are discouraged by the apparently slow progress of all our honest efforts, by the failure of this or the other person, and by the ever new reappearance of enemy powers and their apparent victories, then we should know: the time shall be fulfilled. Because of the noise and activity of the struggle and the work, we often do not hear the hidden gentle sound and movement of the life that is coming into being. But here and there, at hours that are blessed, God lets us feel how he is everywhere at work and how his cause is growing and moving forward. The time is being fulfilled and the light shall shine, perhaps just when it seems to us that the darkness is impenetrable.

Is it true that God only laughs at our efforts and strivings and that all this cannot avail; that we are to receive everything only as a gift? How wonderful is the answer given to us by the mystery of the child! Just as the mother knows that her own surrender, care, and faithful readiness must be present along with God's working and creating, and just as every life comes into being through a deep inward working together of God and man, so it is also in the highest things, in the appearing and breaking through of divine life.

True, it is grace and a gift when our need is relieved and the darkness is illuminated, and it is true that what is best must be given to us and to the whole world, and that we could never produce it ourselves. But we and our efforts always belong to this, even though it were only to keep the manger prepared in which the Child of God wants to lie. Our efforts count, even though like Simeon we only stretch out our arms in the patience of faith and in loyal endurance so that we may receive the holy gift. Even though we only wait, poor and yearning in the darkness, in fervent longing for the proclamation, we are ready, and may help to bring about the fullness of time.

For the miracle of God comes not only from above; it also comes through us; it is also dwelling in us. It has been given to every person, and it lies in every soul as something divine, and it waits. Calling, it waits for the hour when the soul shall open itself, having found its God and its home. When this is so, the soul will not keep its wealth to itself, but will let it flow out into the world. Wherever love proceeds from us and becomes truth, the time is fulfilled. Then the divine life floods through our human relationships and all our works. Then everything that is lonely and scattered and seeking for the way of God shall be bound together by divine power. Then, of human effort and of the divine miracle, shall the world be born in which Christmas is fulfilled as reality.

Only a Rumor

Søren Kierkegaard

*Now when Jesus was born in Bethlehem of Judea in the days of
Herod the king, behold, there came wise men from the east to
Jerusalem, saying, Where is he that is born King of the Jews?
For we have seen his star in the east, and are come to worship
him. When Herod the king had heard these things, he was
troubled, and all Jerusalem with him. And when he had gathered all the chief priests and scribes of the people together, he
demanded of them where Christ should be born.*

MATTHEW 2:1–4

ALTHOUGH THE SCRIBES could explain where the
Messiah should be born, they remained quite unper-
turbed in Jerusalem. They did not accompany the
Wise Men to seek him. Similarly we may know the

whole of Christianity, yet make no *movement*. The power that moved heaven and earth leaves us completely unmoved.

What a difference! The three kings had only a rumor to go by. But it moved them to make that long journey. The scribes were much better informed, much better versed. They sat and studied the Scriptures like so many dons, but it did not make them move. Who had the more truth? The three kings who followed a rumor, or the scribes who remained sitting with all their knowledge?

What a vexation it must have been for the kings, that the scribes who gave them the news they wanted remained quiet in Jerusalem! We are being mocked, the kings might have thought. For indeed what an atrocious self-contradiction that the scribes should have the knowledge and yet remain still. This is as bad as if a person knows all about Christ and his teachings, and his own life expresses the opposite. We are tempted to suppose that such a person wishes to fool us, unless we admit that he is only fooling himself.

The Wise Men

Ernesto Cardenal

The place is Solentiname, an archipelago in Lake Nicaragua; the setting, a campesino church service in the mid-1970s. Padre Cardenal, the priest, does not believe in sermons, but brings the gospel alive by leading his congregation in weekly dialogues like this one:

WE WERE IN THE CHURCH. I said by way of introduction that Matthew's words, "in the days of Herod the King," tell us that Jesus was born under a tyranny. There were three Herods; or, as we might say in Nicaragua, three Somozas: Herod the elder, Herod his son, and a grandson Herod. Herod the elder, the one at the time of Jesus' birth, had ordered

two of his sons to be strangled on suspicion of con-
spiracy, and he also killed one of his wives. At the
time of Jesus' birth he killed more than three hundred public servants on other suspicions of con-
spiracy. So Jesus was born in an atmosphere of
repression and terror. It was known that the Messiah was going to be king, and that's why the wise
men arrived asking for the king of the Jews, meaning
the Messiah.

> Then to Jerusalem came wise men
>   from the East saying:
> "Where is the King of the Jews
>   that has been born?
> For we saw his star in the East
> And we have come here to worship him."

Laureano said: "I think these wise men shit things
up when they went to Herod asking about a liberator. It would be like someone going to Somoza now
to ask him who's going to liberate Nicaragua."

Another of the young men: "The way I figure it,
these wise men were afraid of Herod and didn't want
to do anything without his consent."

Tomás Peña: "They went to ask him for a pass…"

The same young man: "They probably went first to consult Herod because they were afraid of him, and all those people of Jerusalem were filled with fear when they heard talk of a Messiah, just like Nicaraguan people are afraid when they hear talk of liberation. The minute they hear that young people want to liberate those of us who are being exploited, they begin to shake and be afraid. When they hear people say that this government must be overthrown, they shake and are afraid."

Adán: "It seems to me that when those wise men arrived they knew that the Messiah had been born and they thought Herod knew about it and that the Messiah was going to be a member of his family. If he was a king, it was natural that they should go to look for him in Herod's palace. But in that palace there was nothing but corruption and evil, and the Messiah couldn't be born there. He had to be born among the people, poor, in a stable. They learned a lesson there when they saw that the Messiah had not been born in a palace or in the home of some rich person, and that's why they had to go on looking for him some-where else. The Gospel says later that when they left there they saw the star again. That means that when they reached Jerusalem the star wasn't guiding them. They'd lost it."

Félix: "They were confused. And it seems to me that since they were foreigners they didn't know the coun-try very well, and they went to the capital, where the authorities were, to ask about the new leader."

When Herod the king heard this
he was very troubled,
and all the people of Jerusalem also.

Oscar: "I figure that when Herod found out that that king had been born he was furious because he didn't want to stop being the ruler. He was as mad as hell. And he was already figuring out how to get rid of this one like he had got rid of so many already."

Pablo: "He must have felt hatred and envy. Because dictators always think they are gods. They think they're the only ones and they can't let anyone be above them."

Gloria: "And he was probably afraid, too. He had killed a lot of people not long before, and then some gentlemen arrive asking where's the new king."

Félix: "He surely must have put all his police on the alert. I think that's what the Gospel means here: 'He was very troubled.'"

One of the young people: "And the Gospel says that the other people of Jerusalem were also troubled. That means his followers, the big shots, like the Somoza crowd. Because for them it was very bad news that the liberator was arriving. But for poor people it was great news. And the powerful people knew that the Messiah had to be against them."

Old Tomás Peña: "That king who ruled that republic with a firm hand – he ruled a million people or however many there were then – he didn't allow anyone to say anything he didn't like. You could only think the way the government wanted, and they surely didn't allow any talk about messiahs. And they must have been annoyed when outsiders came talking about that, as if they were talking about a new government."

Manuel: "The people had been waiting for that Messiah or liberator for some time. And it's interesting to see that even out of the country the news had got around that he had been born, and these wise men found out, it seems to me, from the people. But in Jerusalem the powerful were entirely ignorant of his birth."

Then the king called
    all the chiefs of the priests
and those who taught the law to the people,
and he asked them where Christ
    was going to be born.

Felipe: "The clergy are summoned by a tyrant who has killed a lot of people. And the clergy answer the call. It seems to me that if they went to his palace it's because they were his supporters, they approved of his murders. Just like today the monsignors who are supporters of the regime that we have. It means that those people were like the people we have today in Nicaragua."

They told him: "In Bethlehem of Judea:
for thus it is written by the prophet."

Don José: "They knew he was going to be born in a little town, among the common people. But they were in Jerusalem, visiting with the powerful and the rich in their palaces. Just like today there are a lot of Church leaders who know that Jesus was born in Bethlehem, and every year they preach about this at Christmas, that Jesus was born poor in a manger, but the places they go to all the time are rich people's houses and palaces."

> When they saw the star again
> They were filled with joy.
> They went into the house;
> they saw the child with Mary his mother,
> and they knelt down and worshipped him.
> Then they opened their boxes
> And they gave him presents of gold,
>   incense, and myrrh.

Tomás: "They come and open their presents – some perfumes and a few things of gold. It doesn't seem as if he got big presents. Because those foreigners that could have brought him a big sack of gold, a whole bunch of coins, or maybe bills, they didn't bring these things. What they brought to him were little things…That's the way we ought to go, poor, humble, the way we are. At least that's what I think."

Olivia: "It's on account of these gifts from the wise men that the rich have the custom of giving presents at Christmas. But they give them to each other."

Marcelino: "The stores are full of Christmas presents in the cities, and they make lots of money. But it's not the festival of the birth of the child Jesus. It's the festival of the birth of the son of King Herod."

Afterwards, being warned in a dream
that they should not return
    to where Herod was,
they returned to their country
    by another way.

Tomás: "The wise men go off by another route. He inspired them not to inform on him, because he was already a fugitive. He made them see they shouldn't go back the same way. It was better to go another way. Already defending his body. At least that's what I think."

Felipe: "By now they were like fugitives too. They went off by another way like they were fleeing. And I think that if they'd returned to the capital they'd have been killed."

Alejandro: "Well, the liberator was born in an atmosphere of persecution, and those who come to see him are also persecuted. The people must have kept the secret…"

Olivia: "The truth is that ever since he was at his mother's breast he had the rich against him. When she was pregnant Mary had sung that her son was coming to dethrone the powerful and to heap good things upon the poor and to leave the rich without a single thing. And from his birth they pursued him to kill him, and then he had to flee in his mother's arms and with his papa…"

Gloria: "Those common people had a hope now. And as soon as they found out he'd been born they felt happy. The neighbors all knew. That star, maybe it was the townspeople talking, and it got to the wise men."

Chael: "Those wise gentlemen found something they weren't expecting – that the liberator was a poor little child, and besides, a little child persecuted by the powerful."

Laureano: "The ones who were persecuting him were the rulers. He was a guy that was coming to change everything, coming to make everybody equal, coming to liberate the poor and to take power away from the rulers because they were shitting everything up. And that's why the powerful went after him to kill him."

The Journey
of the Magi

"A cold coming we had of it,
Just the worst time of year
For a journey, and such a long journey:
The ways deep and the weather sharp,
The very dead of winter."
And the camels galled, sore-footed, refractory,
Lying down in the melting snow.
There were times we regretted
The summer palaces on slopes, the terraces,
And the silken girls bringing sherbet.
Then the camel men cursing and grumbling
And running away, and wanting their liquor
    and women,

And the night-fires going out, and the lack
   of shelters,
And the cities hostile and the towns unfriendly
And the villages dirty and charging high prices:
A hard time we had of it.
At the end we preferred to travel all night,
Sleeping in snatches,
With the voices singing in our ears, saying
That this was all folly.

Then at dawn we came down to a temperate valley,
Wet, below the snow line, smelling of vegetation;
With a running stream and a water mill
   beating the darkness,
And three trees on the low sky,
And an old white horse galloped away
   in the meadow.
Then we came to a tavern with vine-leaves
   over the lintel,
Six hands at an open door dicing for pieces
   of silver,
And feet kicking the empty wineskins.
But there was no information, and so
   we continued

And arrived at evening, not a moment too soon
Finding the place; it was (as you may say)
    satisfactory.

All this was a long time ago, I remember,
And I would do it again, but set down
This set down
This: were we led all that way for
Birth or Death? There was a Birth, certainly,
We had evidence and no doubt. I had seen birth
    and death,
But had thought they were different; this Birth was
Hard and bitter agony for us, like Death, our death.
We returned to our places, these Kingdoms,
But no longer at ease here, in the old dispensation,
With an alien people clutching their gods.
I should be glad of another death.

T. S. ELIOT

The Showing Forth of Christ

John Donne

Lord, now lettest thou thy servant depart in peace, according to thy word: for my eyes have seen thy salvation.

LUKE 2:29–30

THE WHOLE LIFE OF CHRIST was a continual Passion; others die martyrs but Christ was born a martyr. He found a Golgotha, where he was crucified, even in Bethlehem, where he was born; for to his tenderness then the straws were almost as sharp as the thorns after, and the manger as uneasy at first as the cross at last. His birth and his death were but one continual act, and his Christmas day and his Good Friday are but the evening and morning of the same day. And as even his birth is his death, so every action and passage that manifests Christ to us is his birth, for Epiphany is manifestation. Every manifestation of Christ to the world, to the Church, to a particular soul is an Epiphany, a Christmas day.

Now there is nowhere a more evident manifestation of Christ than in that which induced this text, "Lord now lettest thy servant depart in peace..." It had been revealed to Simeon, whose words these are, that he should see Christ before he died. And actually, and really, substantially, essentially, bodily, presentially, personally he does see him. So it is Simeon's Epiphany, Simeon's Christmas day. So also this day, in which we commemorate and celebrate the general Epiphany, the manifestation of Christ to the whole world in his birth, all we, we who besides our interest in the universal Epiphany and manifestation implied in the very day, have this day received the Body and Blood of Christ in his holy and blessed Sacrament, have had another Epiphany, another Christmas day, another manifestation and application of Christ to ourselves. The Church prepares our devotion before Christmas day with four Sundays in Advent, which bring Christ nearer and nearer to us and remind us that he is coming to enable us by a further examination of ourselves to depart in peace, because our eyes have seen his salvation...

To be able to conclude that you have had a Christmas day, a manifestation of Christ in your souls, you shall have a whole Good Friday, a crucifying and an "it is finished," a measure of corrections, and joy in those corrections. You shall have temptations, and a Resurrection and an Ascension, an inchoation and an unremovable possession of heaven itself in this world. Make good your Christmas day, that Christ be born in you, and he who died for you will live with you all the year, and all the years of your lives, and inspire into you, and receive from you at the last gasp, this blessed acclamation, "Lord now lettest thou thy servant depart in peace..."

Simeon waited, says the story, and he waited for the consolation of Israel. And all that God had said should be done was done, for as it is said, "It was revealed unto him, by the Holy Ghost, that he should not see death before he had seen the Lord's Christ," and now he had seen that salvation. Abraham saw this before, but with the eye of faith, and yet rejoiced to see it so, he was glad even of that. Simeon saw it, too…but he saw it with the eye of hope. Of such hope Abraham had no such ground; no particular hope, no promise that he should see the Messiah in his time. Simeon had, and yet he waited, he attended God's leisure. But hope deferred maketh the heart sick (says Solomon). But when that which is desired comes, it is a tree of life. His desire was come; he saw his salvation.

Simeon is so good a servant as that he is content to serve his old master still, in his old place, in this world, but yet he is so good a husband too as that he sees what a gainer he might be if he might be made free by death. If you desire not death (that is the case of very few, to do so in a rectified conscience and without distemper), if you be not equally disposed towards death (that should be the case of all, and yet we are far from condemning all that are not come to that equanimity), yet if you now fear death inordinately, I should fear that your eyes have not seen your salvation today. Who can fear the darkness of death that has had the light of this world and of the next too? Who can fear death this night that has had the Lord of life in his hand today? It is a question of consternation, a question that should strike him who should answer it, dumb (as Christ's question, "Friend, how camest in hither?" did him to whom that was said), which Origen asks in this case, "When will you dare to go out of this world, if you dare not go now, when Christ Jesus has taken you by the hand to lead you out?"

This then is truly to depart in peace by the Gospel of peace to the God of peace. My body is my prison and I would be so obedient to the law as not to break prison. I would not hasten my death by starving or macerating this body. But if this prison be burnt down by continual fevers, or blown down with continual vapors, would any man be so in love with that ground upon which that prison stood as to desire rather to stay there than to go home? Our prisons are fallen, our bodies are dead to many former uses; our palate dead in a tastelessness; our stomach dead in indigestion; our feet dead in a lameness, and our invention in a dullness, and our memory in a forgetfulness. And yet, as a man that should love the ground where his prison stood, we love this clay that was a body in the days of our youth, and but our prison then when it was at its best. We abhor the graves of our bodies, and the body, which in the best vigor thereof was but the grave of the soul, we over-love.

Pharaoh's butler and his baker went both out of prison in a day; and in both cases, Joseph, in the interpretation of their dreams, calls that (their very discharge out of prison) a lifting up of their heads, a kind of preferment. Death raises every man alike, so far as that it delivers every man from his prison, from the encumbrances of this body. Both baker and butler were delivered of their prison, but they passed into divers states after, one to the restitution of his place, the other to an ignominious execution.

Of your prison you shall be delivered whether you will or no. You must die. Fool, this night your soul may be taken from you; and then, what you shall be tomorrow prophesy upon yourself, by that which you have done today. If you did depart from that Table in peace you can depart from this world in peace. And the peace of that Table is to come to it with a contented mind and with an enjoying of those temporal blessings which you have, without macerating yourself, without usurping upon others, without murmuring at God; and to be at that Table in the peace of the Church, without the spirit of contradiction or inquisition, without uncharitableness towards others, without curiosity in yourself; and then to come from that Table with a bosom peace in your own conscience, in that seal of your reconciliation, in that Sacrament; that so, riding at that anchor and in that calm, whether God enlarge your voyage by enlarging your life, or put you into the harbor by the breath, by the breathlessness of death, either way, East or West, you may depart in peace, according to his word, that is, as he shall be pleased to manifest his pleasure upon you.

Love Alone

The Child we seek
doesn't need our gold.
On love, on love alone
he will build his kingdom.
His piercéd hand will hold no scepter,
his haloed head will wear no crown;
his might will not be built
on your toil.
Swifter than lightning
he will soon walk among us.
He will bring us new life
and receive our death,
and the keys to his city
belong to the poor.

GIAN CARLO MENOTTI

The Disarming Child

Jürgen Moltmann

*The people who walked in darkness have seen a great light;
those who dwelt in a land of deep darkness, on them has light
shined...The people will rejoice...For the yoke of their burden
and the staff on their shoulder and the rod of their oppressor
thou hast broken as on the day of Midian. For every boot of the
tramping warrior in battle tumult and every garment rolled in
blood will be burned as fuel for the fire. For to us a child is born,
to us a son is given; and the government will be upon his shoulder, and his name will be called Wonderful Counselor, Mighty
Hero, Everlasting Father, Prince of Peace. Of the increase of
his government and of peace there will be no end, upon the
throne of David, and over his kingdom, to establish it and to
uphold it with justice and righteousness from this time forth and
for evermore. The zeal of the Lord of hosts will do this.*

ISAIAH 9:2–6

THIS MIGHTY VISION of the prophet is founded on the liberation of oppressed men and women through the disarming birth of the divine child. Its goal is the turn from bloody war to the peace that endures and is unbroken. And in order to portray this hope for liberation and peace, the prophet falls back on a picture that is positively expressionist in style. The images jostle and tumble over one another, distorted beyond any possible reality into what is impossible for human beings – possible only to God...

Realistically, though the prophet talks about hunger, slavery and occupying troops, he ends messianically. He lets his vision of the birth of the child and the appearance of the peace of God shine like a light into the conflicts and experiences of real life.

It is not easy to keep these dimensions together when one is used to splitting up faith and politics, God and experience, and when one is accustomed to celebrate Christmas only in the heart and in the bosom of one's own family. But the message of the prophet is a realistic vision, and what it talks about is a visionary reality. It is a message for the people, a message sent into the camps of the exiled, and into the slums of the poor. It is a word against the captains of the arms industry and the fanatics of power. If we really understand what it means, it bursts the bonds of Sunday worship. For if this message really lays hold of us, it leads us to Jesus the liberator, and to the people who live in darkness and who are waiting for him – and for us.

Anyone who belongs to the people who dwell in the land of darkness, or anyone who has ever belonged to it, will find this message about the disarming birth of the child as alluring as it is unbelievable. The people in deep darkness: whom does this mean? In the prophet's time it was that section of Israel that had fallen under Assyrian dictatorship. Every imprisoned Israelite knew the tramp of the invading boots, the bloody coats and the rods of the slave-drivers. Today we can still see Assyrian warriors and overseers like this in the frescoes, with their iron shoes, their cloaks and their sticks. But for the prophet, Assyria is more than just Assyria. She is the representative of the power that is hostile to God, and this makes her at the same time the very quintessence of all inhuman oppression. The prophet looks at the specific plight of his people, but talks about a misery experienced by people everywhere. That is why his words and images are so wide open that prisoners in every age have been able to find in them their own fate and their own hope.

A people in darkness – Isaiah 8 tells us what this means: "They will pass through the land, greatly distressed and hungry; and when they are hungry, they will be enraged and will curse their king and their God, and they will stare up to the sky and look down to the earth, and will find only distress and darkness; for they are in the darkness of fear and wander lost in the darkness." God has hidden his face from them. But instead of waiting for his light, they run to fortune-tellers and mediums, and become more and more confused.

A people in darkness: let me add a personal word here. This phrase touched me directly when in 1945 we were driven in endless and desolate columns into the prisoner-of-war camps, the sticks of the guards at our sides, with hungry stomachs and empty hearts and curses on our lips. But many of us then, and I was one, glimpsed the light that radiates from the divine child. This light did not allow me to perish. This hope kept us alive.

A people in darkness: today I see before me the millions of the imprisoned, the exiled, the deported, the tortured and the silenced everywhere in the world where people are pushed into this darkness. The important point is not the nations, which can be accused of these things. What is important is the worldwide brotherhood of the men and women who are living in darkness. For it is on them that this divine light now shines.

Peoples in darkness: how that cries out today from the Third World in Africa and Asia, and from the Third World in our own country – cries out for liberation and human rights! The struggle for power and for oil and for weapons ruins the weak, enriches the wealthy, and gives power to the powerful. This divided world is increasingly capable of turning into a universal prison camp. And we are faced with the burning question: on which side of the barbed wire are we living, and at whose cost? The people in darkness sees the great light. To this people – to them first of all – the light shines in all its brightness. To these people the child is born, for the peace of us all. Do we belong to this people, or do we cling to our

own lights, our fortune-tellers and our own interpreters of the signs of the times, people who tell us
what we want to hear, from Nostradamus and astro-
logical calendars down to the learned interpreters of
the laws of history?...

More is promised here than can be expressed simply through old-soldier reminiscences. For God's victory does not come about through new armaments
and force levied against force, or through alliances
and solidarity. God has his own, divine kind of victory. For God's victory puts an end to all human wars
and victories once and for all. It is a final victory,
which serves peace, not one that leads to the next
war, as our melancholy victories usually do. The
prophet gives his images of war so alien an orienta-
tion that they actually describe the conquest of war.
Every weapon becomes a flame, every aggression fuel
for the fire. God's victory puts a final end to the victories of human beings. People lose their taste for
them. Swords are turned into ploughshares and
peace treaties replace the atom bombs.

But how is this supposed to happen? Does not the
power to liberate the masses stem from rifles just as
much as the forces of oppression? How can oppres-

sion and war be fought against and overcome with-out bringing new oppressions and new wars into the world, again with bloody coats and the tramp of boots through the streets?

All the images the prophet uses to paint the possible future point to one fact: the birth of the divine child. The burning of the weapons, the jubilation and the great lights are all caught up in the birth of God's peace-bringer. They are all to be found in him. Now the prophet stops talking in intoxicating images and thrilling comparisons, and comes to the heart of the matter: the person of the divine liberator. "To us a child is born. To us a son is given." This future is wholly and entirely God's initiative. That is why it is so totally different from our human plans and possibilities. If liberation and peace are bound up with the birth of a little helpless and defenseless child, then their future lies in the hands of God alone. On the human side, all we can see here is weakness and helplessness. It is not the pride and strength of the grown man which are proclaimed on the threshold of the kingdom, but the defenseless-ness and the hope of the child.

The kingdom of peace comes through a child, and liberation is bestowed on the people who become as children: disarmingly defenseless, disarming through their defenselessness, and making others defenseless because they themselves are so disarming.

After the prophet's mighty visions of the destruction of all power and the forceful annihilation of all coercion, we are now suddenly face to face with this inconspicuous child. It sounds so paradoxical that some interpreters have assumed that this is a later interpolation. The prisoners who have to fight for their rights also find it difficult to understand how this child can help them. But it is really quite logical. For what the prophet says about the eternal peace of God which satisfies our longings can only come to meet us, whether we are frightened slaves or aggressive masters, in the form of the child. A child is defenseless. A child is innocent. A child is the beginning of a new life. His defenselessness makes our armaments superfluous. We can put away the rifles and open our clenched fists. His innocence redeems us from the curse of the evil act that is bound to breed ever more evil. We no longer have to go on like this. And his birth opens up for us the future of a life in peace that is different from all life hitherto, since that life was bound up with death.

"For to us a child is born. To us a son is given. The government is upon his shoulders." The liberator becomes a pleading child in our world, armed to the teeth as it is. And this child will become the liberator for the new world of peace. That is why his rule means life, not death; peace, not war; freedom, not oppression. This sovereignty lies on the defenseless, innocent and hopeful shoulders of this child.

This makes our fresh start into the future meaningful and possible. The oppressed will be free from oppression. And they will also be free from the dreams of darkness, the visions of revenge. They stand up and rejoice, and their rejoicing frees their masters too from their brutal armaments. The oppressors with their cudgels, their iron shoes and their bloody coats will be freed from their grim machinations and will leave the poor in peace. For the new human being has been born, and a new humanity will be possible, a humanity which no longer knows either masters or slaves, either oppressed or oppressors. This is God's initiative on behalf of his betrayed and tormented humanity. "The zeal of the Lord of hosts will do this." It is the zeal of his ardent love.

There is no other initiative we can seize with absolute assurance, for ourselves or for other people. There is no other zeal for the liberation of the world in which we can place a certain hope.

There are certainly many other movements, and much fervent zeal for the liberation of the masses. It certainly sounds more realistic for people in darkness to dream of God's day of vengeance, finding satisfaction in the hope that at the Last Judgment all the godless enemies who oppress us here will be cast into hellfire. But what kind of blessedness is it that luxuriates in revenge and needs the groans of the damned as background to its own joy? To us a child is born, not an embittered old man. God in a child, not as hangman. That is why he prayed on his cross: "Father, forgive them; for they know not what they do." It sounded more heroic when, forty years ago, in 1934, Hitler's columns marched through Tübingen, singing with fanatical zeal: "One day, the day of revenge. One day, and we shall be free." It was a zeal that led to Auschwitz and Stalingrad...

Emperors have always liked to be called emperors of peace, from Augustus down to the present day. Their opponents and the heroes of the people have always liked to be called "liberators," from Arminius of the Cherusci to Simón Bolívar. They have come and gone. Neither their rule nor their liberation endured. God was not with them. Their zeal was not the zeal of the Lord. They did not disarm this divided world. They could not forgive the guilt, because they themselves were not innocent. Their hope did not bring new life. So let them go their way. Let us deny them our complete obedience. "To us this child is born." The divine liberty lies upon his shoulders.

What does his rule look like? We have to know this if we want to begin to live with him. He will establish "peace on earth," we are told, and he will "uphold peace with justice and with righteousness." But how can peace go together with justice? What we are familiar with is generally peace based on injustice, and justice based on conflict. The life of justice is struggle. Among us, peace and justice are divided by the struggle for power. The so-called "law of the strongest" destroys justice and right. The weakness of the peacemakers makes peace fragile. It is only in the zeal of love that what power has separated can be put together again: in a just peace and in the right to peace.

This love does not mean accepting breaches of justice "for the sake of peace," as we say. But it does not mean, either, breaking someone else's peace for the sake of our own rights. Peace and righteousness will only kiss and be one when the *new person* is born, and God the Lord, who has created all things, arrives at his just rights in his creation. When God is God in the world, then no one will want to be anyone else's Lord and God anymore…

But is this really possible here and now, or is it just a dream?

There is nothing against dreams if they are good ones. The prophet gave the people in darkness, and us, this unforgettable dream. We should remain true to it. But he could only see the shadowy outline of the name of the divine child, born for the freedom of the world; he called him Wonderful Counselor, Mighty Hero, Everlasting Father, Prince of Peace.

The New Testament proclaims to us the person himself. He is Jesus Christ, the child in the manger, the preacher on the mount, the tormented man on the cross, the risen liberator.

So according to the New Testament the dream of a liberator, and the dream of peace, is not merely a dream. The liberator is already present and his power is already among us. We can follow him, even today making visible something of the peace, liberty and righteousness of the kingdom that he will complete. It is no longer impossible. It has become possible for us in fellowship with him. Let us share in his new creation of the world and – born again to a living hope – live as new men and women.

The zeal of the Lord be with us all.

Sources and Acknowledgments

November 24: From Christoph Friedrich Blumhardt, *Action in Waiting*. Farmington, PA: Plough, 1998.

November 25: Sylvia Plath, "Black Rook in Rainy Weather," from *Crossing the Water: Transitional Poems*, copyright ©1960 by Ted Hughes. Reprinted by permission of HarperCollins Publishers, Inc., and Faber & Faber.

November 26: J. B. Phillips, "The Christian Year," from *Good News: Thoughts on God and Man*, copyright © 1963, The Macmillan Co., New York.

November 27: Friedrich Foerster, "Father, Son, and Holy Ghost," from *Christ and the Human Life*, copyright © 1953, Philosophical Library, Inc., New York.

November 28: "A Spirituality of Waiting," by Henri J. M. Nouwen in *The Weavings Reader*, ed. by John S. Mogabgab. Copyright © 1993 by The Upper Room. Used by permission of Upper Room Books.

November 29: Bernard of Clairvaux, "Annunciation Dialogue," from *The Living Testament: The Essential Writings of Christianity Since the Bible*, Harper and Row, 1985.

November 30: "The Annunciation," from *Amazing Grace* by Kathleen Norris, copyright ©1998 by Kathleen Norris. Used by permission of Riverhead Books, a division of Penguin Putnam, Inc., and Janklow & Nesbit.

December 1: From *Meister Eckhart, from Whom God Hid Nothing*, edited by David O'Neal. © 1996 by David O'Neal. Reprinted by arrangement with Shambhala Publications, Inc., Boston, www.shambhala. com.

December 2: Thomas Aquinas, *Lauda Sion Salvatorem*, transl. Laurence Swinyard, Baerenreiter Ausgabe 481a. Kassel: Baerenreiter Verlag, 1958; and Karl Rahner, "The God Who Is to Come," from *Encounters with Silence*, (translated by James M. Demske), St. Augustine's Press, South Bend, IN 1999, / Copyright by The Newman Press, originally published by Verlag Felizian Rauch, Innsbruck, Austria (first edition in 1938), as *Worte ins Schweigen*. Reprinted with permission. N.B.: The verses by Aquinas did not preface Rahner's original text but were added by the editors of this volume.

December 3: From Isaac Penington, *Select Essays on Religious Subjects*. Philadelphia: Joseph Crukshank, 1783.

December 4: Reprinted from Madeleine L'Engle, *Bright Evening Star*. Copyright ©1997 by Crosswicks, Inc. Used by permission of WaterBrook Press, Colorado Springs, CO. All rights reserved.

SOURCES

December 5: From Alfred Delp, "The Shaking Reality of Advent," in *When the Time Was Fulfilled*, Farmington, PA: Plough, 1965; originally from Alfred Delp, *Zwischen Welt und Gott*. Frankfurt am Main: Verlag Joseph Knecht, 1957. Printed with permission of the publisher.

December 6: From Loretta Ross-Gotta, *Letters from the Holy Ground*. Franklin, WI: Sheed & Ward, 2000. Reprinted by permission of Sheed & Ward, an Apostolate of the Priests of the Sacred Heart, 7373 S. Lovers Lane Road, Franklin, WI 53132.

December 7: From William Stringfellow, "Advent as a Penitential Season," from *A Keeper of the Word*, edited by Bill Wylie Kellermann, Wm. B. Eerdmans, copyright ©1994. Reprinted with permission.

December 8: From J. Heinrich Arnold, *Discipleship: Living for Christ in the Daily Grind*. Farmington, PA: Plough, 1995; and *The Writings of Edith Stein*, transl. Hilda Graef, quoted in Mary Ann Simcoe, ed., *A Christmas Sourcebook*, Liturgy Training Publications, 1999.

December 9: From an unpublished address by Philip Britts (Isla Margarita, Paraguay, December 12, 1948) in the Bruderhof Archives, Rifton, New York.

December 10: "Mosiac of the Nativity: Serbia, Winter 1993," copyright 1996 by the Estate of Jane Kenyon. Reprinted from *Otherwise: New & Selected Poems* with the permission of Graywolf Press, Saint Paul, Minnesota.

December 11: From *The Original Revolution* by John Howard Yoder. Scottdale, PA: Herald Press, 1971. Used with permission.

December 12: From Emmy Arnold, "Christmas Joy," from *When the Time Was Fulfilled*. Farmington, PA: Plough, 1965.

December 13: From Karl Barth, "Lukas 1:5–23," from *Predigten 1917*, pp. 423–431 of the original German version; Copyright © Theologischer Verlag Zürich, 1999. Translated by Robert J. Sherman. Reprinted with permission.

December 14: From an address by Oscar Romero, December 24, 1978, as reprinted in Oscar Romero, *The Violence of Love*. Farmington, PA, Plough, 1998. The piece by William Willimon is Copyright 1988 Christian Century Foundation. Reprinted by permission from the Dec. 21–28, 1988, issue of the *Christian Century*. Subscriptions: $42/yr. (36 issues), from P.O. Box 378, Mt. Morris, IL 61054, 1-800-208-4097. N.B.: The verse from Romero did not preface Willimon's original text but was added by the editors of this volume.

December 15: Based on various unpublished sources spoken or written by the author during Advent 2001.

SOURCES

December 16: From *Evensong* by Gail Godwin, copyright ©1999 by Gail Godwin. Used by permission of Ballantine Books, a division of Random House, Inc., and John Hawkins & Associates, Inc.

December 17: From Leonardo Boff, "The Man Who Is God," from *Jesus Christ Liberator*, copyright © Orbis Books, 1978. Reprinted with permission.

December 18: From "The Wreck of the Deutschland," in *Poems of Gerard Manley Hopkins*, Oxford University Press Ltd., 1948; and Evelyn Underhill, *Light of Christ*, Harrisburg, PA: Morehouse, 1982. Reprinted by permission of Morehouse Publishing, Harrisburg, Pennsylvania and Continuum International Publishing Group, Ltd. N.B.: The verse from Hopkins did not preface Underhill's original text but was added by the editors of this volume.

December 19: From *Dorothy Day: Selected Writings*, edited by Robert Ellsberg. Copyright © 1983, 1992 by Robert Ellsberg and Tamar Hennessey. Published in 1992 by Orbis Books, Maryknoll, NY 10545. Reprinted with permission.

December 20: From Brennan Manning, "The Shipwrecked at the Stable," from *Lion and Lamb: The Relentless Tenderness of Jesus*, copyright © Chosen Books, a division of Baker Book House, 1986. Reprinted with permission.

December 21: From Dietrich Bonhoeffer, "The Coming of Jesus in Our Midst," from *A Testament to Freedom, The Essential Writings of Dietrich Bonhoeffer*, edited by Geoffrey B. Kelly and F. Burton Nelson, Harper San Francisco, 1995. Reprinted with permission.

December 22: From Romano Guardini, *The Lord*. Washington, D.C., Regnery, 1954. Copyright © 1954. All rights reserved. Reprinted by special permission of Regnery Publishing, Inc., Washington, D.C.

December 23: From *For the Time Being* by Annie Dillard. Copyright © 1999 by Annie Dillard. Used by permission of Alfred A. Knopf, a division of Random House, Inc., and Russell & Volkening as agents for the author.

December 24: From Martin Luther, "Sermon for Christmas Day; Luke 2:1–14" (1521–22) in *The Sermons of Martin Luther*. Minneapolis, MN: Lutherans in All Lands Press, 1906.

December 25: From John Chrysostom, "The Joys of Christmas," from *The Living Testament: The Essential Writings of Christianity Since the Bible*. New York: Harper and Row, 1985.

December 26: From Giovanni Papini, *Life of Christ*, translated by Dorothy Canfield Fisher, copyright © Harcourt, Brace and Co., 1925.

SOURCES

December 27: From *On Earth as in Heaven* by Dorothee Soelle. ©1993 Dorothee Soelle. Used by permission of Westminister John Knox Press.

December 28: From *God in the Dock* by C. S. Lewis copyright © C. S. Lewis Pte. Ltd. 1970. Extract reprinted by permission.

December 29: From Gustavo Gutiérrez, *The God of Life*, Orbis, 1991. Reprinted with permission.

December 30: From *The Jesus I Never Knew* by Philip D. Yancey. Zondervan, 1995. Copyright © 1995 by Philip Yancey. Used by permission of Zondervan.

December 31: Jane Tyson Clement, "The Master," in *No One Can Stem the Tide*, Farmington, PA: Plough, 2000; and Thomas Merton, from *Raids on the Unspeakable*, copyright © 1966 by The Abbey of Gethsemani, Inc. Reprinted by permission of New Directions Publishing Corp. and Laurence Pollinger Ltd. N.B.: Clement's poem did not preface Merton's original text but was added by the editors of this volume.

January 1: From Eberhard Arnold, "When the Time Was Fulfilled," from *When the Time Was Fulfilled*, Farmington, PA: Plough, 1965.

January 2: From *Meditations from Kierkegaard*, translated and edited by T.H. Croxall, copyright © James Nisbet and Co, Ltd., 1955.

January 3: From Ernesto Cardenal, *The Gospel in Solentiname*, vol. 1, translated by Donald D. Walsh, copyright © Orbis Books, 1976. Reprinted with permission.

January 4: "The Journey of the Magi" from *Collected Poems 1909–1962* by T.S. Eliot, copyright 1936 by Harcourt, Inc., copyright © 1964 by T.S. Eliot, reprinted by permission of the publisher and by Faber & Faber.

January 5: From John Donne, "The Showing Forth of Christ," from *The Showing Forth of Christ*, New York: Harper and Row, 1964.

January 6: From Gian Carlo Menotti, *Amahl and the Night Visitors*, copyright © G. Schirmer, 1950.

January 7: "The Disarming Child," from *The Power of the Powerless*, by Jürgen Moltmann. English translation copyright © by SCM Press Ltd. Reprinted by permission of HarperCollins Publishers, Inc., and SCM Press, London.

Index of Authors

INDEX

INDEX

BREAD
AND
WINE

Readings
for
Lent
and
Easter

Arnold ♦ Augustine ♦ Berry ♦ Buechner ♦ Chesterton
Eckhart ♦ Gibran ♦ Kazin ♦ Kierkegaard ♦ Merton
Muggeridge ♦ Nouwen ♦ Pascal ♦ Romero ♦ Rossetti
Sayers ♦ Tolstoy ♦ Updike ♦ Wilde ♦ Yancey ♦ and others

If you liked
Watch for the Light
you should have the
companion volume…

BREAD AND WINE
READINGS FOR LENT
AND EASTER

. . . .

LIKE **C**HRISTMAS, Easter is trivialized by the culture at large. But for believers, it is not just another holiday, but central to our faith. Each year, millions focus on the real meaning of the season by marking the days of Lent, a season of soul-searching and spiritual preparation, a time for reading and reflection.

Experience Lent and Easter like never before with this collection of pithy and challenging daily thoughts from the world's great spiritual writers and poets. *Bread and Wine* follows the same format as *Watch for the Light*, with the same integrity and diversity. Includes writings by Thomas à Kempis, Johann Christoph Arnold, Dietrich Bonhoeffer, Frederick Buechner, Oswald Chambers, G. K. Chesterton, Alfred Kazin, Jane Kenyon, Søren Kierkegaard, Thomas Merton, Henri Nouwen, Blaise Pascal, Christina Rossetti, Dorothy Sayers, Edith Stein, John Updike, Walter Wangerin, William Willimon, Philip Yancey, and others.

The best read-aloud Christmas stories of all time

HOME FOR CHRISTMAS
STORIES FOR YOUNG
AND OLD

. . . .

THEY ARE SOME of the most cherished childhood memories, those unhurried December evenings when the family gathered around the fireplace, lighted tree, or dinner table to hear father or mother read that favorite Christmas story.

This anthology contains twenty truly exceptional stories that you and your children will want to hear again year after year.

Some are time-tested favorites from the world's most beloved children's authors – Pearl Buck, Selma Lagerlöf, Ruth Sawyer, Elizabeth Goudge, Rebecca Caudill, Henry Van Dyke, and Madeleine L'Engle. Others are little-known European tales not available in English anywhere else.

Selected for their literary quality, insight, and spiritual value, they will resonate with people of all ages. Handsomely illustrated by David G. Klein.